FINDING God's Voice in the Noise

FINDING God's Voice in the Noise

PAM APFELBECK

PAM APFELBECK PUBLISHING

FINDING God's Voice in the Noise

Copyright © 2023 by Pam Apfelbeck

ISBN: 978-1-7376944-2-7

Published by Pam Apfelbeck Publishing

All rights reserved. No part of this book may be reproduced or utilized in any form or by any means, electronic or mechanical, or by any information storage and retrieval system—except for brief quotations for the purpose of review, without written permission from the publisher.

Cover design: Canva modified by Pam Apfelbeck

Cover inspiration: Andrea, Amanda, Calandra, Mike

Interior design & typography: Pam Apfelbeck

Inspiration for this book was birthed through Content Conspiracy coaching and workshops from Andrea Dell, High Octane Marketing, LLC. To learn more visit www.andreadell.com.

For more information about finding God amid confusion, visit www.pammyjo.com and subscribe to my newsletter.

DEDICATION

This book is dedicated to souls who are not yet *confident* about their connection to God's Spirit of Truth, and about how to identify "God's words" or "energy" within us.

It's also for believers who want a deeper connection and CONVINCING understanding of WHY IT'S WORTH the time to consciously connect to God.

Why does this ability to connect exist and why do we want to work at a deeper, clearer level? Because of "noise" (distractions) in ourselves and the world around us. These distractions are interfering with our answers, our happiness, and the peace that is our birthright.

Some souls recognize the inward work of the Holy Spirit because they were taught about it in church or from loved ones, or from reading the Bible. Some people aren't sure what it feels like inside us or know how to recognize confidently that it is God's Voice.

Uncertainty makes us feel inadequate about our understanding or suspicious when others talk about this Holy Spirit connection. "Hearing God's Voice" is not the same as religion or believing we're eternal spirits in human bodies (with no accountability or Divine Leadership).

The way to be in touch with God's Voice is to understand God's heart. Then we stop evaluating and looking around for God, and the "invisible" God will become recognizable.

This book is also dedicated to my family, who've watched my struggle to find God's Voice and find my purpose, amidst the noise and struggles in my own life.

God bless you all!

INTRODUCTION

On September 18, 1996, I walked away from everything that mattered to me: a full time federal job at the USDA Forest Service. My career was important to me, and this one was supposed to be the source of all the income and benefits for my three daughters and me for the rest of my working life.

Looking back, it was no surprise I ended up with this scary decision of leaving, because three years after I started with the Forest Service, in 1984, stressors began to amp up. I got divorced in 1987 and became a single parent of three beautiful daughters. But I thought my career was safe, even three years AFTER that, when I met a man 60 miles away in Orofino, Idaho (where I was born, and my first daughter was born).

This man, Mike, and I dated for a year before I considered relocating. He owned property and lived near his mom, so he wouldn't consider moving. Then in 1991, a year after we started dating, I DID secure a job in Orofino.

But moving to Orofino to be near Mike was the start of a "career fiasco" loading itself onto a trailer and moving with us! Only three MORE years after I went to all the trouble to switch jobs to be with Mike, I got notified (1994) because of "workforce management," my job was being eliminated.

WHAT?! I was "the provider" for my girls! They couldn't eliminate my job! Sure, we lived with Mike, but we kept our finances separate, having both been divorced and each having our own children to support (him a son, me three daughters).

The ELIMINATION OF MY PERMANENT FEDERAL JOB left me resentful because the manager had earlier promised she "had me in mind" for a promotion. But instead of a promotion, what she was able to deliver was the loss both of my job AND the potential promotion one.

I didn't leave the agency just then. I accepted a job commuting out of town 60 miles back to my former office in Grangeville. If only I'd only stayed in Grangeville, I'd still have a job, and I began to question if meeting Mike had been the best thing for us.

My duties in Grangeville were wonderful and so was working for my favorite supervisor, but a 70-minute commute each way and being gone 12 hours a day wasn't easy on any of us. It couldn't go on forever, but it beat nothing, plus when I committed for one year, both Forest Supervisors promised me a job in Orofino when one opened.

During that year, my absence began affect my family. Me being gone that long became a strain on our kids, on Mike, and on me. I'd get home after long workdays and be too exhausted to cook and to listen to the kids' needs. THUS, when a job closer came up only 45 minutes away in Kooskia, I reluctantly accepted—reluctant because I didn't have a great feeling about the duties. But I was again promised I'd be hired in Orofino when a job opened, so I thought this was a temporary situation.

However, after I went to work at Kooskia, a job DID open in Orofino, but they gave the job to someone else. I resented this, too, and began to realize that I DIDN'T MATTER to them!

Meanwhile, things in Kooskia were NOT going well. When I'd accepted the jo, they promised I'd only do technical work. They didn't need me at their busy reception desk up front. I'd stay in the back at my desk doing finance and purchasing only. I was good at technical duties but hated reception and payroll.

After a few days on the job, my supervisor walking in my office and said I was doing payroll, saying the lady at reception was "too busy to keep up with it." She handled all the personnel work and payroll is part of that, but they took it away from her and gave it to me, having lied to me.

Shortly after that, they also assigned me recreation duties, accounting for thousands of dollars of campground receipts. They had a Resource Assistant who should be handling recreation duties, but they took that away from her and gave it to me. All of that, with all my technical duties, left me with a desk piled high, constant interruptions, and frustrations that made this job opposite of the one I did SUPER well in Grangeville, even with a long commute.

After a year in this horrible job, the "last straw" fell. I walked by my supervisor's office one day and heard my two co-workers' and my supervisor say my name. One was the receptionist who was too busy for payroll. She said, "If only we could get Pam comfortable up front, I could go on fire assignments. But I don't know how to make her be willing!"

Hearting that, I froze in the hall, before I got to the doorway. I let it sink in to be sure I heard right. They kept talking about me, laughing about how hard it was to get Pam to do things. So I kept walking like a zombie past that doorway to drop off outgoing mail, and as I came back by, I stopped, looked at them, said nothing, and walked back to my overflowing desk.

I still didn't want to admit it to myself what they were doing, because of my dependence on a federal salary, but something in me knew that day that THIS office and working with THESE people was HOPELESS.

Not long after that, another task was added, confusing demands made, and as I sat at a computer to research a report I needed, I froze again. My brain went blank. My lips moved by themselves, declaring "I'm done." I went back to my office, picked up my purse, lunch, and jacket and walked up front. I stopped at the office of my only co-worker there, waved goodbye, and drove home.

As soon as I got home, the phone started ringing repeatedly. It was the remaining co-worker trying to "counsel" me. I don't know why she would since she was one of the three plotting to overwhelm me. After she finally stopped calling, a forester from that office called me and said, "I don't know what you said to her, but law enforcement is all over this office and in

Orofino at the main one. They said you threatened to shoot three people, and we're in lockdown!"

This fiasco went on for days. I was warned NOT to approach either office. Meanwhile, the Forest Service called in a "crisis counselor" to help Kooskia deal with "the trauma of a threat." (It so happens the counselor was the one they sent ME to when I said I couldn't keep up with piled on work, so she already knew me well).

That counselor called me AFTER she met with them at my office and said, "Don't go back to work! They've gone nuts, and it's a hostile work environment for you!"

But I didn't resign with all these false accusations hanging over me. I couldn't let them destroy me, but before I could go back to work, I was required to meet with law enforcement. They ruled that this was only an "incident" without basis, NOT AN ACTUAL THREAT.

Though I could have filed a grievance or sued them then, I chose to go back to redeem my reputation and to look them calmly and politely in the eye. However, a few months later, when nothing had changed, no one was willing to help, and Mike and I had talked, I left for good. Mike decided, "It's time for you to leave that chicken shit outfit."

So, on September 18, 1996, I calmly packed up my things, drove STRAIGHT to talk the administrative officer in Orofino, and announced I wanted to resign/retire. I asked him to ensure there was NO REPEAT of the reputation damaging hysteria, drama, and harassment like last time. He agreed and guaranteed it. He said if he could mediate, he would, but they wished my supervisor would retire and blamed her for it. Still, I resigned, rolled my retirement into an IRA, and left my career 17 years sooner than I'd planned.

As soon as the realization hit of what I'd done, four years of self-loathing became my main meal, and I could NOT forgive myself. I felt like the most *worthless* parent who had ever lived. Justified or not, I'd bungled an entire federal career, sabotaged my finances, and ruined my girls' futures.

But this became a bigger decision than a career one! Since I no longer HAD my career to lean on, all I did have (besides family) was God. Or did I? Did I still believe in a God Who would let this happen to us? I doubted I even knew God, and I definitely distrusted myself.

It was odd that I didn't trust God because I used to. I remembered when my faith started in childhood, when I accepted Jesus Christ as my savior (and that I had a need for one, so I could know and be close to God). My faith escalated at age 22 when our mom became very ill, and I had to move back home to my parents' ranch to take care of her. I started going to my childhood church to cope with Mom's condition.

My sister, Lois, also did and suddenly something hit her from the Holy Spirit–the revelation that she had the gift of prophecy. She spoke to those around her direct words from God, and all of it seemed accurate and uplifted their souls. That was fine with me! I looked up to my sisters. But then one day she spoke prophesy to me, and informed me that I, TOO, had the gift of prophecy, and God would speak through me.

Oh, no He won't, I thought. I'd rather become an atheist and run the other way! I wanted NOTHING to do with the notion, although I accepted that Someone DID speak through her, and that the Someone probably WAS God. Still, that wasn't for me! But she was a determined woman and insisted I "try it," because she was certain I also had that gift.

Terrified but obedient, I began to make recordings for loved ones, as thoughts and words seemed to stream through me that described traits about others that were helpful for them to hear. Whether that Someone who spoke through me was God or my imagination, I wasn't sure. And not knowing TERRIFIED me, because the WORST thing I could imagine being was a FALSE PROPHET who spoke lies in the name of God Almighty.

We prophesied that Mom would be healed. After she died, I decided I WAS a fake. But before I could "give up on" the gift, I prophesied to a loved one that "what has been impossible will be possible, and you will have a son." She didn't. That cemented my flight from prophesy!

EXCEPT, 20 years later the lady never got pregnant but her daughter, who could NOT get pregnant, DID, and she had a son. I started sweating when the loved one told me that God was talking to her offspring, not to her. It was her daughter who couldn't get pregnant but miraculously would. AND NOW DID, and had a healthy son as prophesied by me.

Suddenly live, human EVIDENCE that it was God in me hit at precisely the time in my life I needed to find faith again. That little baby boy was a SIGN! But I still preferred to run from God and wasn't sure He still wanted me. If He did, He'd need to prove it in a way I would have NO MORE DOUBTS.

Because I still had a lot of doubts about ME, and having no career wasn't the paradise I expected! Mike had to work more hours. I was home to deal with my kids instead of ignoring them most of the week, so they'd figure it out on their own.

So, one evening when no matter what I did they were unhappy, it got to me. After sobbing in our bedroom for an hour, about bedtime I needed OUT of the house alone. It was a stupid day to leave because it had rained all day for days with no let up! Visibility sucked, even with the wipers on high, and a thick fog covered the entire Clearwater valley.

I drove off anyway, figuring the weather fit my mood, and drove up a steep grade toward the ranch where I'd grown up on Upper Fords Creek Road. The first third was windy, steep, sharp corners, and I hated the road, but I felt drawn to drive there. I passed Dead Man's Curve, where one slick winter when the plow hadn't passed my school bus almost slid backwards into Fords Creek and killed us all. (It earned its nickname).

I finally got to the top of the grade to a wide overlook where one could see, in good weather, the long, deep Clearwater River valley far below. But that day I couldn't see anything, so I let the car run, because if not I'd get cold AND feel like I was drowning in the dark, deafening rain.

I felt deathly alone, and tears poured out of me as I saw nothing but the voluminous rain pouring onto the wipers. Suddenly my heart felt a desperate urge and I got an idea. I'd ASK God for a SIGN! If He didn't answer, I'd go home and accept myself for the loser I was and let this "God" thing go. (I didn't expect God to answer, but at least it would settle the issue.)

Between sobs, I looked up past the car's roof, beyond the storm, away from earth, and screamed toward Heaven, "IF this WAS You in me; if I know You and am not crazy or imagining things; if I really AM a prophet with Your Word in me, **PART THESE CLOUDS OVER MY HEAD!"**

I felt FOOLISH. God wouldn't do such a thing, not for someone like me, so I laid my head on the side window and cried as the wipers swiped back and forth like a river was flowing over them.

As I waited in despair, I wondered why I'd been so certain in childhood I believed in God. I'd gladly accepted that Jesus embodied God, and God raised His body from the dead to defeat eternal death. I knew He'd done it so human souls could approach God again, after walking away from Him and calling Him a liar eons ago. If God raised a body after it was three days dead, He could love me and forgive my mistakes.

I realized I believed in God and Jesus not so much to avoid condemnation as to forgive myself for being imperfect. Still, on this cold, wet night after all my failures, I didn't believe friendship with God was an option. He might forgive me, but maybe He was no longer up for sharing Himself with me, IF He ever had!

A sound in the car brought me back from my thoughts, and it was so different that I sat up in the seat I'd leaned back to cry in. What was that SOUND? Oh. The wipers were squeaking. Why do wipers squeak? I held my breath, opened my eyes, and stared at the windshield. There were no water drops on it. The wipers were wiping dry glass.

I turned them off, but it didn't sink in why they weren't needed until I looked out my side window and saw something I could NOT BELIEVE WAS THERE: **black sky with hundreds of twinkling stars!**

I threw the car door open, leaped out, and looked straight up. ALL around and above me in a circle was a clear, beautiful sky, but outside this circle in every direction were clouds and that thick, foggy mist as far as I could see, up and down the valley.

"You parted the clouds!" I screamed. Then I cried, jumped, and laughed. With my arms raised high to Heaven I yelled, "Oh, thank God in Heaven! I'm NOT an imposter! I really DO know THE God!!"

I drove home that night a different person, even though I'd lost my benefits, income, and my career, I'd gained something because of the loss: Certainty about God. He SO IMPRESSED me that day I've studied with Him ever since, and I'm NOT letting Him go again!

God then sent me to church for prayer and sent Jesus to teach me about the Bible and to introduce me more intimately to God as a Person. God and I have read the Bible together for 26 years and He's shown me the true meaning of Bible passages, which brought the Bible TO LIFE IN MY LIFE.

God also showed me, by how He treats me, WHY He encourages us to connect with Him, why families in the Bible did, and how doing so changed their lives and their fate.

After a few months of hearing from God, writing with God, and having Jesus and God speak to others through me, I came to RECOGNIZE God's "Voice." All the clutter and confusion, accusations, and rantings I'd heard STEPPED ASIDE when the Voice of the Almighty came to talk to me.

I went back to work in two local jobs after walking away from the feds, but in 2018 I was called BACK to serve God full time. I joined two major human healing lifestyles: Unstoppable Influence™ and the Code Red Lifestyle™.

Unstoppable Influence™ is spirit and soul healing and learning to love and accept yourself and your eternal nature. It teaches to answer your callings from God—do what you came to earth to do (and BE you!). It helped me reclaim my state of mind and amped up my connection to God even more. Code Red Lifestyle™ is to heal your body by eating REAL food, drinking water, and sleeping. It reclaimed Mike and my health so we can think clearly and be active.

Finding God's Voice in the Noise is my third book. My first was My Yahweh Journey: How I Became One with I AM. It's about how God and I built our relationship. It really happened AFTER what I share here about finding God.
https://www.amazon.com/dp/1737694409

Romancing an Angel of THE Lord shares Mike and my story living under God as a couple, and it explains how MUCH God solidified our friendship and gave us peace with each other. https://www.amazon.com/dp/1737694417.

In this book you'll learn to relate to and connect with the real God and read evidence that you already have the connection ability BUILT INTO you! Half of the "secret" is believing the connection exists. Your PURPOSE and the CALLINGS for your life you long for are waiting for deeper exploration, as you collaborate with God to strengthen them.

The Bible is full of stories of HOW God activated people's connection to Him, WHY they decided to, and how they learned to respond and trust that part of themselves who connects to THE God.

You can do it, or do it more fully, too.

It's your birthright!

CHAPTER 1: Jesus with Me

My first memory of Jesus was hearing grandma thank Him, frequently whispering after each breath, "Thank You, Jesus." And again, "Thank You, Jesus."

I took Him somewhat for granted after that as a part of life and didn't think I needed to do or be any different.

That changed when I was four or five and, having not attended church much because we lived far out in the country on a busy ranch, I heard the words Sunday School and was told I was going.

I was terrified because "school" was a dreadful thing that tore my older sisters away from home, so I didn't get to see them.

Having them come home crying from school and hearing their stories about how they felt mistreated and picked on by teachers (and called names by other students) made it seem evil and creepy.

Being told about this "Sunday school" ON THE WEEKEND when sisters are finally home, gave me a tummy ache, and I didn't want to go!

But one Sunday, someone took me to town so I could go to church, but instead of sitting with Grandma like I thought I should, I had to go to Sunday school with a bunch of kids I didn't know. Then we did a thing called "Bible study."

I'd never touched the Bible except to stroke the pretty page edges and feel the fabric of Grandma's, and I couldn't read. I felt uncomfortable around all these strange kids and wanted to go home. At home I could wade in the rivulets of water racing down the driveway during late spring snowmelt. I could jump for joy watching the gushing water wash away the ice, as the sun shone down to help it melt. That was the only form of "study" I needed!

Miserable in this tiny classroom full of kids, I squirmed in rebellion. The first question the teacher asked was, "Who remembers which ___ was the one who ___ from last week's Bible lesson?"

Last week? A "lesson?" What is that? I panicked, feeling BEHIND and stupid. "Grinning Sunday Schoolers," who'd been there for weeks studying, raised their hands to be first to spout the correct answer.

After I saw that everyone there knew the answer to this AND the next question except me, I felt like NOTHING, an incomplete person, and the stupidest child to ever live. I decided that Sunday or any form of school wasn't right for me.

Because, after all, do the birds ask which one sang the last song before the next bird can sing? Do cows raise their hooves to ask permission to moo next? Do water droplets wait their turn to melt off the snowbank and race down the driveway? Must they account for who went before them before they can run?

And who cares who did this or that, what his or her name was? What was that to me, and what could I learn from it?

I did not go back to Sunday School because I could not compete with those already taught and felt ignorant and bad there because of it. I still believed in Jesus but was not interested in memorization. It had never been easy for me to memorize, only to understand. I understood the Bible was real, but it began to feel like just another textbook I didn't wish to be forced to read.

Later my attitude about learning more about Jesus changed, as I grew up and began to get into tough fixes, where I needed help when no human was around. At those times I'd look around and say, "If there is a God or if Jesus hears, please help me." I didn't demand help, but I asked for it.

Did help come? I think so. I think it must have, because somewhere along there I began to believe there was a God. I think I believed it because of that help and those answers I "blindly" accepted when they came.

Before I hit pre-teen, I'd picked up this "imaginary boyfriend" who went with me whenever I'd walk alone. I was out roaming on the ranch a lot and had all sorts of conversations with this fellow. But I THOUGHT this fellow was just a neighbor boy I was having "pretend" conversations with. IF SO, he had sure known what to say to make me feel good and loved!

It was inconvenient, though, when I saw my actual neighbor boy, because he'd say NOTHING to me—he was that bashful. After seeing him I was always confused. Why was he so quiet then but not when I was alone in my head with him? Later in life I was shown Who that really was keeping me company, and Who helped me accept myself and keep caring about living.

Though I didn't go back to Sunday School I did go to church, and one Sunday they were talking about sin and the need to be forgiven for it. I wasn't sure if I had it, and if I did, I didn't think I wanted it, so I preferred to be forgiven.

If accepting Jesus was the answer to keep me out of trouble, especially after Grandma thanked Him so often, I'd go for it. I proclaimed that I believed in the Lord Jesus Christ and that God raised Him from the dead, after He paid the price for ALL our sins.

I was not SURE what all my sins were, but I knew I had them. Was it the time I wrote on a wall with fingernail polish, and Mom saw it and blamed visiting children, without asking if I did it? (And I didn't correct her out of fear?)

Or was it when my brother was riding on the back of my trike, I lost control on the slope of the porch, and we fell off backwards with the trike on top of us? And that cute little 2-year-old boy broke his tiny arm, and it was my doing. Was that a sin? According to my brother, for the rest of our lives, YES, it was a sin, and an unforgiven one.

For a long time, I still wasn't sure what sin meant. Was it me kicking and screaming about getting my hair permed and wearing dresses to school, to the point I refused to go? I had to be convinced Mom and Dad would go to jail if I didn't go, so I went. Was THAT a sin?

To avoid sinning, did I have to deny what I was to obey my parents? Probably. And IF my sin was covered, why did I still get in trouble or get tempted to do sneaky stuff and sin again? And why did people still fight about things after being forgiven for doing so?

I felt saved, but still flawed and full of mistakes. I did commit my heart to believe in God AND felt peace usually at church (with Grandma).

Then in high school, a biology teacher's claims inspired me to DEFEND God! He was teaching the theory of evolution (as a "chance" happening) to the class and forcing us to believe it.

He was a cruel, arrogant, sarcastic, and insulting critic of those who believe in Creation. He called those who believe in Creation "naïve" and claimed the "scientific evidence" disproved God or Creation.

That moment is when I realized I sure as crap DID believe in God. And their theory of "chance improvements" or "advancing complexity" seemed much more of a myth than the idea of intentional design did! I also didn't understand what gave him the right to arrogantly judge believers.

So, I argued the logic of "chance improvement" with him, and alongside me was my agnostic best friend who later became an attorney. For us logical thinkers, that teacher's "accidental" theory was far easier to argue against than believing in a Power beyond our comprehension!

Yet, despite how I believed, it still made me doubt a little bit when I hit college. Some classmates realized this was their first chance to rebel, and they did it right in front of my face.

Just like in high school, I was accused of being naïve and made fun of because I didn't "get" their dirty jokes. They also pressured me to get drunk, and they justified sleeping around.

Though I felt out of place with them, I also felt uneasy around those who were raised religiously and "stuck with" their church gatherings and lifestyles, but they didn't intermingle with the other college kids. It was like the "nonbelievers" were infectious or something.

Believers also wouldn't accept me UNLESS I attended their church services AND became active in volunteer groups or activities. It felt like I had to "prove" my belief to them and live by their social rules, or else I was "one of those to be avoided."

So, I was accused either of not being religious enough by those socially organized and in strict attendance of church activities. Or I was called an "ice queen" by the party animals in college. Once again, just like in Sunday school, high school, and any other group I'd been near, I didn't fit anyone's mold UNLESS I did something I did not believe in doing!

On top of that, my femininity was questioned. The biology teacher in high school was also my German teacher. As if to really strike my match on fire, when assigning German names to us, he called me a masculine name: Helmut. When I protested, he would not back off. It's as if he realized I doubted the wholeness of my femininity.

He hoped to shame me by calling me that name, but I have since looked up what it means related to the Bible and in German. It means "brave hero." God is the One who showed me the meaning, and no matter how femininity is measured, I am a hero who is not ashamed.

But back in high school and college, my faith wavered. All those arrogant insults and pressure to fit in succeeded in making me unsure of WHAT I believed.

Could they be right? Could everything on the planet be by "chance?" If so, where did order and process come from—out of nowhere?

And why did I have to be EITHER a wild party animal OR a demur church-going Christian? WHY COULDN'T I just be me and hang out with my "Imaginary Friend?"

Since those days, I took a writing course where a teacher said that when sharing a story, "SHOW, DON'T TELL." **I realized I had needed SHOWN, not told, that God is real.**

And in 1997 when I was desperate, after losing my career and had asked God to show me, HE DID! He parted the clouds and stopped the rain. God knew how to show me and what question I could ask that would convince me.

After that I realized my "imaginary friend" growing up was not a boyfriend or a neighbor. He WAS the Spirit of Truth that was in Jesus. He was a form of Jesus that God sent to walk with me to keep me from feeling lonely, to enjoy God's creation, and get to know God's Spirit as a friend and companion.

Before I realized this, I had thought of God's Spirit as some intimidating force that descends without feeling and overpowers me. But Jesus and the Spirit of Truth have no desire to overpower anyone. They come to us so that we feel accepted as we are and don't feel alone.

GOD WITH ME

After I lost my federal job in 1996, I wasn't sure God was anywhere near me, despite my Jesus beliefs. Because I was so unsure of God, after I returned to church out of desperation, God sent Jesus, because I trusted Jesus and was open to Him.

But eventually God showed up, too. On April 21, 1997, I went to the altar for prayer for pain in my back. When I got home, I recorded this experience in my journal. Here it is!

"My eyes are closed, and I hear music and feel it soak through me. I exhale because tension has built. The pastor comes to me, and I feel his arms on my back, but I can't move even though I'm sobbing. I'm too relaxed. I don't know why I'm sobbing, so I say, "Father God, whatever I have is Yours, whether You heal me or not."

The pastor said, "Father God, reveal to Pam a picture of how You see her."

I had laid down by the altar because the power was so relaxing, and I saw only a cloud. A voice said, "Lay still and wait." The singers sang a song I'd not heard for years, and I thanked God for it.

Then God spoke. "You are a stone, clear and smooth and pure, like a diamond, but with many colors radiating and reflecting off you. When people look at you, they see reflections of themselves the way I see them, the way they wish to be.

"Your heart is like a window, clean and pure, with no grime or mud or smear on its surface. When people look at your heart, they look through you and see Me.

"I will mute your mouth at certain times, when I wish to speak, and you'll know Me by the golden light I show you, like the light you see now."

I saw a yellow light and nothing else. Then something began prickling my skull, like tiny electrical shocks. My ears heard hundreds of them crackling.

I heard the choir sing a song again from old times, but this one was in perfect harmony, with only a few quiet instruments playing.

Later, I mentioned the old-time gospel songs they sang second. One of my daughters said, "What old song?" Then I asked my sisters and neither remembered a second song. I finally called and asked the music director, who said they only sang ONE song, the first one.

The second one, the one in perfect harmony, no one else heard. It was angels. I heard Heavenly angels singing.

But God wasn't done with me at church or at the altar. Even after saying ALL that about how He saw me and how He'd make use of me, He sent his Son nine days later.

On April 30, 1997, after the sermon, I went up for prayer. With my eyes closed I invited Jesus into the garden of my heart. I was feeling so much turmoil, I moaned. There was pain in my loins, abdomen, and chest. I was writhing, my knees were shaking, and I began groaning and crying.

I was scared and felt hopeless, so I shouted, "Shepherd!" (My nickname for Jesus). I saw Him, with a scythe in one hand, a huge, sharp hoe in the other, and He began thrashing. It happened so fast, I felt only pain.

But I heard Him SHOUT once, "No, she's MY Garden! I come to the Garden ALONE!!" Furious then (with fervor He moved), he shouted at demons, and grabbed roots of something in my heart, flailing them out the door while catching and throwing out others.

It was an extra body experience!

He was especially pissed at the one he called "Death-and-Despair" (also named "Suicide") and was particularly rough with it. He kept shouting, "MY Garden, get out! Mine alone!"

Jesus was awesome, a champion, a Lion. He was a Shepherd with napalm. Whoa, can He move!

Someone prayed for joy while He was furious. I jumped. Someone prayed, "Fill her, Lord," and I bounced in the air. Shepherd's aim was true, His Love unfailing. He made me laugh, and I did. Some others there praying wailed right then.

Why did Jesus come? Why did God send Him for this hands-on cleansing experience? It's because I committed myself to God the previous prayer, when God spoke to my mind and cleared it electrically.

The Shepherd (the Son of God) came to clear my heart, to get her ready for God's service, because the Garden of my heart belongs to God. He created it. And He shares it with His Son.

CHAPTER 2: Jesus Alone

Jesus was half God and half human here on earth and was used to being near God. To restore that feeling He went off "alone" on earth to connect with God and put distance between Himself and the heart cries of the Chosen.

Who are "The Chosen?" They are those set aside for His Father's Kingdom, close to His Father's heart, who have not believed and purchased the lies that the so-called "prince" of lies has traded in.

Lies swap places with the truth, to distract and separate the Chosen from the One who made them in Love. Jesus is a long-time witness to Soul Trading, the currency of the spirits.

His followers worried about the currency of the Romans, the currency of the elders, the doves in the temples. His concern is the trading of souls, the dirtying of souls. This appalls Him because of the value of souls to His Father, to Him, and to those loyal to the truth.

THE SON CRIES OUT TO GOD

One day when He was still on earth, this weighed on Him as He woke at sunrise. He hiked to the peak of the mountain before His followers knew He was gone.

"Father, I grieve for them. They so easily and calmly hear lies about how doing what the elders say will bring them close to You!" And He recalls their open hearts accepting and believing lies about what they must DO to be 'good with God.'

The scriptures had shown them, "For I desire mercy, not sacrifice, and acknowledgment of God rather than burnt offerings." (Hosea 6:6)

"Father, they STILL believe that those who are sick and hurting are so because they are evil and sinning against You! But it's the glumness and draining of their strength from the demands put on them that makes them ill, not 'sin.'

"I wish we could heal them all this time that You've given Me to be Jesus of Nazareth. I wish we could end death, illness, and fear now, instead of waiting for the rest of The Chosen to be born and to eventually choose truth!"

He nods as He looks up and out to where He knows God is standing, as He reads God's feelings.

"Now's not the time, I know." He admits. "More souls must be given time to live, thrive, suffer, and find their faith and their belief that they're eternal spirits who know You. I know. I don't like it, but I know."

Jesus sighs, wishing He could do more now without keeping future generations of humans from existing on earth. But now's not the time.

He still feels frustrated that He can't do more. And He looks ahead to what He knows is coming for Him. He must live, feel, and be part of all the trials, pain, and hardship that people face when they agree to live as a human soul.

"My bones now feel their twisted joints and their aching pains. My lungs feel their short, panicked breathing. My Spirit wishes we could intercede in all ways. Yet I know I can't because then they'd not learn and grow strength and resolve.

"I don't mean to renege on our arrangement here in my body, as a human. Even I feel the temptation to do it all and fix it all RIGHT NOW. It's a powerful and sneaky temptation!

"Yet I know it's not really a 'god complex.' It's not a belief we ARE all, we can do all, without regard for the free will we and others have. This existence as a human makes one forget the troubles that shortcuts would bring to others and turn them into dependents, instead of steadfast spiritual people in human bodies.

"OH, I must go now, Father. Some of our friends have found Me. There they are climbing the hill! I love them, but I miss You. I need You to quickly strengthen me, so I don't speak before I must or act when I must not.

"You are all I have here to give me strength. Please flood me with Your thoughts and wisdom, while I have a few more minutes alone."

THE FATHER ANSWERS

"Son, you're my arm, my justice, and my compassion. It is okay to feel what you feel and okay to wish you could take all their pain away. Better you feel that way than feel gleeful about manipulating them or 'fixing' them, so you'd feel 'good' about yourself!

"I have never left You (here or previously when we worked together). I am always with You, whether on earth or in our home. And you know I'll be in the deepest of low places with you! I AM always with you and will not let you fail!

"Let's talk together if you're not sure what you're feeling or seeing. You'll never make a wrong decision, but if you want help trusting yourself, I AM here to listen and reassure you.

"Those who will come after You, those who believe in truth and know we brought them to life, will never make missteps that can't be righted. They won't feel emotions that are evil. They may not understand many times why they feel what they feel, but their steps will lead them to the places they need to go.

"And they will be your legacy—they will inherit your estate! And you will be theirs because they will have access to your awesome resources any time they ask! You are passing on the kingdom you and I built over to them.

"As they get to know you, they'll want to be your friends and learn from you. And with a little luck, they will like you enough they will choose to learn from me, AND from each other and themselves. Their reward for trusting the truth about us, and themselves, is they will make themselves able to accept eternity as a gift from us.

"Look, here come your friends! Even when they don't believe you, shine for them. When they don't understand, explain to them. But do not feel the need to control them, because they're worthy and able to each be themselves, and thrive no matter the situation or lesson they're learning.

"I trust you, Son. Now trust them. It's not only that I've chosen them, or you've chosen them. They've chosen us, too."

FRIENDS ARRIVE

"Master, did we offend you, that you needed to leave us?" they asked.

"No, John, no Peter," Jesus said. "Mary, you look lovely this morning. Where is Martha?"

"She started breakfast and is now pacing the kitchen waiting for you. Come on, Master. Hurry back to her."

"Why do you call me master?" Jesus asked. "It's time to call me friend. Because I've just found out we are all friends of the Father. That's why I came to this mountain alone, to talk with our Father and get reassurances and clarifications for today."

"It's time for you to also meet with our Father, one-on-one, for your strength, instructions, and encouragement for the day! Father will help you keep these bodies calm, let go of the last day's worries or hardships, and turn concerns over to Him. This cleanses and renews your spirit, like bathing helps us feel fresh and new," Jesus said.

"But we have You, Big Friend, and being with You cleanses us," Mary said.

"We don't need the Father!" said Peter. "Let God rule Heaven. We are here with You. And knowing You makes us strong. We will overcome these Romans without even a sword! Because when more people hear of Your strength, knowledge, ability to heal, and that even demons fear You, we will take back our land from these invaders without a fight!"

John disagreed. "No, it is your love which will deliver us, Friend Jesus. We are your true family, we who worship and follow and love you. Because even your family is not sure what to think of you, but we love you and will do anything for you."

Jesus looked at them. "My friends, you don't realize now what you say or what is coming that will test your resolve and scatter you, one from another. That's why you MUST learn to trust the Heavenly Father and seek His will, even on earth, even in these lifetimes! You must.

"I'll not be with you in body for all time, I will be with you in Spirit, and it is the Spirit you must learn to trust and commune with.

"You can come up on the mountain, away from the distractions and noise, the troubles around you. Or you can find that peace within by focusing your mind despite noise. But finding the Father's Spirit of Truth is something you must learn to do," Jesus told them.

"Let me help coach you while I am here to hold your arm, or to offer you a hug and reassurance to take some of the strain off you. But DO start now learning this quiet connection. I am always with you, but not always here like this," Jesus said.

Just then Mary, Peter, and John stepped aside to talk while the others chatted with Jesus. "What does He mean? Nothing can slay or stop Him. He's proven that with the elders, who oppressed us with unfair rules about our worth and how only they can make us clean," Peter said.

"Isn't He here to deliver us from these earthly rulers and destroy them with a touch? Why is He telling us to connect with The Name (The God, YHWH) instead? Why would He say that?" Peter asked. "Have we disappointed him in some way?"

"No, we cannot disappoint Him, because He is love," John answered.

Mary nodded. "Yes," she said, "He will conquer evil with His love!"

CHAPTER 3: Good or Evil?

Questioning God is something people forget they can do. God likes to be in conversations and likes to answer questions.

He's also okay with people asking for proof He exists. God prefers we ask over guessing about things.

QUESTIONS ABOUT GOD

1) Why choose God and decide there's an omnipotent (unlimited power), omnipresent (existing everywhere) Force or Source who created everything that exists, including us?

2) If God exists, why do we care? Why should we know His name, communicate with Him, or care what He thinks?

3) Did God create standards of behavior or rules of existence as He created everything? If so, if we run amuck of those rules or ignore and deny God exists, what happens to us?

4) If we accept God exists, where did God come from? If God existed everywhere, why DID God increase even more to make us, when God already had or was everything?

5) If God is everything and we're part of that, why don't we already know what is "best" or that there is a "best?" If we don't, will something we DO or BE cause us to stop existing or to exist miserably?

THE ANSWERS

God didn't care to be alone because that got boring and God wanted life to be interesting, so God decided to make others. Before making others, God divided His Essence into parts. Then God made others to entertain and interact with the parts.

But interacting with others can either feel motivating OR irritating. Either way, at least having others to interact with is a challenge.

Put another way, God was lonely, so God made offspring and wanted the offspring to have friends.

Why should we care that God exists? Because since we came from God, we can learn about ourselves from interacting with God. God made interacting a way to learn about ourselves and enjoy the variety in all the others. God made us to discover our differences, our uniqueness, and our similarities, to appreciate that variety exists.

Does God have standards? Yes. God is creative. Behaviors that destroy others' integrity go against God's goals and hopes for variety and growth, and for existence to be interesting.

God decided it is not interesting to be controlled or feel controlled, by having choice taken away.

Yet it's uninteresting to have no variety—to be limited and never expand, learn, and experience differences or newness.

So, God created many things, many ways to feel, many types of thinking, and many characteristics. God is not boring. Neither is Creation.

DEFINE EVIL

Evil is damaging the integrity of others by interfering with their rights to exist, to learn, or to explore. Interference from others puts people into disarray.

"Disarray" means to throw (someone or something) into a state of disorganization or untidiness. To strip and confuse.

IT MAKES ANOTHER FEEL NAKED, EXPOSED, AND UNPROTECTED.

For example, if a satellite receiver, radio, or cell phone is in disarray, it cannot tune to its signal and function. It's in a state of static and signal loss. It emits only NOISE.

DEFINE GOOD

Good is to promote the health, growth, and integrity of yourself and others. Respect that God divided up and made others for a purpose and allow that purpose to reveal itself to them.

If you input into it, do it in a way they have free will, can say no, and can choose their own next steps.

Good does not exist at the expense of others and doesn't need to control others. Good does not exhaust other people's resources (steal or destroy). Good values other people's resources.

DEFINE CONDEMNATION
(An Automatic Consequence of Evil)

The consequence of evil, of harming others, comes back around, and you become disarrayed and lose your own integrity. What you want to "do to" others will come back and "do to you!"

"Do unto others as you would have them do unto you." Jesus Christ (Luke 6:31).

So, condemnation is the consequence of destroying others' rights to exist, grow, learn, and have integrity (hold themselves together, be real.)

It is the result of interfering with people's ability to put themselves back together if they feel they are falling apart.

Condemnation is more impactful if you are the one that causes them to feel disarrayed (fall apart, distrust themselves, feel distraught) because you were the one who planted these false beliefs in them.

IN SUMMARY, the consequence of harming others is for the harm to circle back on oneself and make one become disarrayed. To lose integrity (no longer be held together, to recognize oneself accurately) is the consequence (the judgment) for evil choices or behaviors.

DEFINE REDEMPTION
(The Automatic Consequence of Good)

Redemption is the PROMISE or provision (process, remedy, guaranteed cure) to heal those who are disarrayed, who were snagged and dragged into others' vortexes or upheavals.

Redemption makes one whole again by healing the disintegrations of integrity. You can be stripped of all your confidence and lose all faith in yourself or God, and yet be re-created.

You are redeemed when you realize you are on the path to wholeness, to completely accepting yourself as you were intentionally created, and be what you want to be as a person.

GOD VS. SATAN: CHOOSE GOD

Choose God, because with God, you can be whole (fend off the results of errant behavior that tear up your integrity) by moving toward wholeness. By connecting to God—to the Source of your original existence, you choose to receive God's healing waves that put you back to your whole self and hold you together there.

God cannot disintegrate or lose integrity because God is integrity, just like water cannot be dry because it's wet. Like water, God can be a cloud or vapor or unseen (like moisture content of the air), but God cannot be a void (dry—with no moisture).

OR BE STUCK WITH "SATAN"

Choose Satan (accusing and harming yourself and others), and in so doing, become more and more disintegrated, lose your true makeup, and be sucked into the crumbling disintegration of others you've helped cause as they fall apart.

As they fall apart, they will suck parts of you with them. If you REALLY want to fall apart yourself, forget who you once were, and be trapped in a cycle of disintegration, then choose lies, harm, anger, greed, and then lust after the downfall of others.

In doing so, you will lose yourself.

QUESTIONING GOD!

Question 1: Why should we believe You are an omnipotent (unlimited power), omnipresent (existing everywhere) Source who created everything that exists, including us and our physical and spiritual environment?

GOD: Because I exist, you do. You're proof I exist. The intricacies of Creation prove design was involved.

Question 2: If God exists, why do we care? Why know or communicate with God or care what God thinks?

GOD: Because I know you and know how to keep you existing effectively.

Question 3: Did You create standards of behavior or rules of existence when You created everything? Can we run amuck of those rules if we ignore or deny they exist, and what happens if we do?

GOD: YES. Realities exist that hold the universe together, for it to exist with integrity. If you defy or willingly ignore those realities, consequences come.

It is like driving a highway, but you decide to make your own route by driving through trees or over boulders. There will be consequences for your car (and you). Think of your body and soul as the car, and the highway as a place you can travel without crashing and hurting.

Question 4: IF You exist, where did You come from? If You existed everywhere, and time is not affecting your continuation, why DID You increase what You already were (to make all of us), when you were already "everything?" That's VERY confusing!

GOD: I've always been and always will be, but I prefer sharing Myself with others rather than sitting around being "everything" alone. Interacting with, watching, and sharing feelings and thoughts from others I call "interesting." Being the only one I call boring.

"It is not good to be alone." I said that when I decided to make a suitable companion for Adam. I said it because I knew and felt it already, and I knew Adam felt the same. But it was not enough that he knew just any companion–Adam needed an INTERESTING and DIFFERENT one.

Question 5: If You ARE everything and we're part of that, why don't we already know what is "best" or that there is a best for us? AND Will something we DO or BE cause us to stop existing or to exist miserably?

GOD: You don't know (yet) what is "best" because now you must spend time learning and making choices! You need free will (which involves learning and making decisions). That way, you're more than robots or mindless slaves or machines.

You deserve the right to make your existence decline and become boring or upsetting, so that when you make it interesting and uplifting you can hold onto that and appreciate it. You'll learn the difference and choose what you want.

Free will is for the sake of variety and learning. Have you ever gotten children a puzzle they put together, then had them ask if there was a different puzzle or toy available?

Have you watched a movie or TV episode once, maybe twice, and then been irritated when the same movie or episode came on right after it? Did you change the channel or advance the episode, because it was too boring to relive the same story that soon after?

Being creative by nature means you (and I) want variety. Free will allows it. Free will creates it. Slavery or robotic life makes existence repetitive. Eventually it drains one's creativity and begins to diminish existence. That's the process called "death."

CHAPTER 4: Intuition

What is intuition, and why care what it is or what we do with it? Intuition is a connection point. It's a receiving point built into our natures and into our spirit. Our physical body can sense it, too.

Connecting our intuition to God Almighty (Creator/Source) gives us peace and clears the noise out of our eternal energy. It also relaxes our body.

We were made to connect with God, and the process by which we do so has been called intuition. Some people call it the Holy Spirit descending on you or being anointed. That's fine, but there is a lot of misconception about it when it's called intuition.

My intuition is strong, and my connection to God is strong, because I went out by myself, utterly desperate. I'd lost my job, my career, and it felt like I was losing family connections. People weren't safe emotionally near me, and I was not safe emotionally.

I went out by myself, opened that connection up – my heart, we call it, and God came down and sat in me.

To open myself up, I did it desperately, LOUDLY, and alone, because I COULD NOT FIND ANYONE TO HELP me. I felt I had NO choice but to assertively ask that God help me.

Having God respond and sit in me was the ultimate thrill, and the most peaceful experience I've ever had! There's nothing as good as when God was sitting in me.

Because of how MUCH I enjoyed feeling One with God, I serve God freely out of choice, because God has become a solid rock who helps me with EVERYTHING.

For example, God knew I wanted to write this book, but I got writer's block. I had a loved one who narrated her book and recorded it. I decided to speak out some chapters in video format to overcome my block like she did. It worked!

God inspired her to share HER experience with me, to help get me a solution. This coach is my daughter, Andrea Dell, who wrote "Dream Client Gold Mine" during one of the worst traumas of her life!

SOMETIMES my intuition works better if I speak things out (do a video), narrate to myself, OR talk to a friend. It helps to "get out of my head" and ALLOW intuition to burst forth.

To fine tune their understanding of intuition and get confidence recognizing it, some ask God for signs or help, and for what the next steps are.

And it's even a SIGN that we DO have intuition that we desire to "find our next steps!" Why do we even desire them? So that we can develop our intuition that is burning within us, to be used and integrated into our hearts and minds.

See, intuition is a native skill. It's a latent, automatic, natural, eternal ability to connect to God. It's a binding and an automatic connection center, where we are designed to connect with God Almighty's power.

What does "binding" mean? A binding agreement or promise is an obligation that can't be broken. If you decide you want to connect to God, it will become, when you accept it:

1. Something that just happens without conscious effort.

2. Something that nothing can undo or foil unless you step away from it or it gets interference. It's your CONTRACT with God, and nothing can break it!

Then WHY would we (intentionally or unknowingly) step away from it? Because if we don't connect to God's power, we'll connect somewhere else, because it's part of our basic core need. We'll find a way to connect to SOMETHING to fill the void.

The absence of using intuition, or using it to only connect to others in our circle or distractions in the world, will develop a HABIT in us. We'll get used to attempting to get our energy, strength, and feeling of belonging through others only (not God's power).

This will EVENTUALLY drain us, because they or that habit won't be enough, like any addiction that needs more and more to fulfill the "need" or make us feel "high."

Relying and using whatever distraction in the form of another person will also drain them, because "getting" what we need from someone else sucks some of their energy, strength, or time. Up to a point, they may feel OKAY about it. They might even FEED off our need to connect. But past that point, it will become too much for them. They'll either resent us and accuse us, or they'll walk quietly away to avoid us.

And if we connect to a habit rather than a mentor or loved one, it will stop being enough over time, because it's NOT filling us up or giving us healthy answers and mapping out our future.

Instead, it's a distraction technique whose payoff to us will eventually stop working (or bore us almost to death) AND make us feel guilty and unfulfilled, like there is SOMETHING MORE to life we're not doing.

TO SUMMARIZE:

Everyone needs to belong and connect, and that is good. But relying on another for answers past that point may be too much for people and make them secretly dread our company or interactions.

One should HOPE they either walk away OR you realize it, because if you are depending on someone else, and it's NOT too much for them, then you may wish you weren't close to them at all!

Because IF they are okay that you get your self-worth or answers ONLY from them, then they are "feeding on" your neediness. They are getting too much of their (supposed) self-worth from meeting your needs!

This may sound harmless, but the trouble is, what if their answers don't meet your needs because they're not seeing you through God's eyes (you as you really are, what you really need right now)?

What if they are feeding off your insecurities (instead of helping you heal and get secure) so you will need them even more?

Also, what if they just say what they feel like saying, or say what they THINK you need to hear? And this goes on and on with no progress, growth, healing, or answers that lead you somewhere?

God is DIFFERENT. God's power is multi-faceted: it sees all sides and versions of us. It's also multi-colored: all the different emotions we need addressed are present and available.

God's parts recognize your parts, understand what's within you, and know how to connect to you to find the answers or healing you need.

Put another way, since God is the Source of all things, God accurately recognizes what we feel and (really) need. Plus, God doesn't need to "feed" on us. God sees the truth of what we're feeling or what's happening with us. He KNOWS us.

God never has a "need to be needed" agenda. Thus, with God, we have TRUST.

When we need sympathy, we get it from God. When we need strength, God's strength helps strengthen us. If we need to talk to someone to find peace, God will lead us to what we REALLY need to deal with, so we find AUTHENTIC peace (not just an emotional Band-Aid on a wound that will reopen later and fester).

Also, God doesn't have to be "in the mood," rested, or have time to cope with OUR PARTICULAR NEED, so that He just throws something out there to appease us or waits to find time on His schedule. Omnipresent means the calendar is always open!

So, there's no guilt that we're "bothering" God or taking time away from someone else. There's no fear that we can't fully explain what we need, especially when we're not sure. And there's no concern God will run out of time for us, or we'll have to renew the coaching contract next year.

None of that. No fear. No daggers of guilt and doubt. God is accessible and fully equipped for you only, for you uniquely!

HOW TO "OPEN UP" INTUITION

Intuition is important, was hard for us to define, but is REAL. For intuition to be opened and recognized, it needs to be acknowledged. Admit it's there, even if you don't know what it feels like or how to use it.

There is a lot of learning involved. At first, when I became aware of "God's Voice" connecting to me, I ran and hid from it. But later, because of DESPERATION in my life, I cried out to God for help and "opened up" for answers.

By ASKING for God's help (desperately), I acknowledged that I needed it and had the means to receive it, AND I was determined to hear or see the help.

So, to get the connection working, we must open the intuition center like a flower opening in the morning to allow the sun (for us, the Son of God or Light of Truth) to shine on it.

If we close all up or get anxious, it can prevent the reception, as if you turned the knob away from a radio station or switched your TV to a static channel.

For me, I have enough practice that God's Spirit knows me. It knows where to find me (knows my state of mind and what I need to hear). And if I don't reject it (give up) or hide from it (go into negative rants/downward spirals OR distract myself with something), it will come as soon as I call it.

IT'S NOT THAT I DON'T GO INTO LOW PLACES AND HIDE. It's that when I'm ready to be open again, God's ALWAYS there, and Intuition (a Divine gift and ability) is ready.

When I'm open, that's my intuition desiring my Creator, so I can receive strength, acceptance, ideas, forgiveness, hope, a new outlook, or whatever else I need to receive, or that I need to switch out mentally or in my heart.

Sometimes I just need Someone to feel what I feel or help me figure out how to do something, or where to find something. I "lose" my coffee cup a lot, and when I speak, "Where's my cup?" my eyes SEE it before I can finish the sentence!

Life isn't perfect. I don't "find intuition" all the time. Sometimes I can't hear God. BUT, even if I don't, I serve God out of choice, whether I get instant connection with God right that second or not.

I recently asked myself WHY I choose to connect with God long-term. It's to KEEP AFTER that connection. It's like a car when it's rarely started gets a rundown battery. I want to keep my confidence over the connection healthy and my soul battery charged.

WHY ELSE continue to connect with the eternal? Because God has become a solid rock who helps me with everything. When I'm swept away in a flood of despair or I'm frustrated, that Rock is a place to step out of the mire and get some air. It's a place to rinse off and dry off from the thick dark soup that feels like it might drown me.

Sometimes it takes reaching out to someone with my voice, like with the friend who narrated a book before writing it. Yes, my intuition sometimes wants to be HEARD instead of written or as thoughts in my head. It wants to manifest itself outside of my brain by speaking it out or talking to a friend.

Sometimes it wants to share itself with another, so it doesn't feel alone (like writing to yourself in a journal can feel alone).

God isn't jealous that we want to be heard by others rather than talk to Him or His Spirit directly. At times that's what we need, so we have some variety with who hears our intuition, and a chance to connect with other people.

And sometimes God uses other people to transmit to our intuition. He encourages their intuition by letting it help give us answers. THAT is another reason to acknowledge and work with our intuition center–to let other people's intuition help us and let us help them.

HOW TO RECOGNIZE INTUITION

REMEMBER, Intuition is not a myth and not something that can be used by someone else. It's a connection of our energy to God's energy, where God connects to our mind and heart and teaches us.

He also sends us signs and signals about what our next steps are or lets the answers we need show up for us. Intuition helps us recognize the answers when they come.

How intuition works can be different for different people, or even different for one person at different times.

- Some people have dreams or thoughts that just show up.

- Some talk to someone else, and the ideas or answers flow out of them suddenly.

- Some "know" or "feel" what they want to come, and it comes.

- Some "hear" or "sense" God's voice.

In my case, the Word of God usually comes to me, but I also get signs like certain words someone speaks (or posts) JUST after I asked a question or had a thought about it.

I know it's not the person really saying it! It's God saying it through them. It's reassuring to realize God's on top of things and has people He can call in to help YOU get answers.

Your intuition is what recognizes the answers because it can "see" God's help or signs! Isn't this amazing?!

A lot of things "leap out at me." During my first year of learning about "signs," God's Presence, and God's voice, I'd see the same three numbers on EVERY car license I saw on the road! It pretty much freaked me out. I felt like I was either dreaming OR had died and wasn't really on earth.

But then someone in a store would SAY something which exactly fit what I was wondering about.

Or I'll lose something, look ALL over for it, and can't find it. Then I pray about it, forget to look for it, and either I suddenly remember where I put it or find it when not looking! (Many times, my head turns toward it and my eyes latch onto it. It's freaky!)

Since intuition is built into our spirit to connect us to God, why do some people not even know what it is? And why do some people come up with a lot of bad decisions in life? Why can't we just "hear" or discern the signal?

I found that answer because I've been in a program called the Unstoppable Influence Academy™ with Richard and Natasha Hazlett. It included access to a monthly book club. One of the book club selections, Born to Win, really resonated with me when I was looking for this answer.

JUST as I was asking God, "How do I explain this?" (Why do intuition and wisdom get corrupted?), that month's book selection answered it THE SAME WEEK I SOUGHT THE ANSWER!

It's because lies substitute for the truth! Zig and Tom Ziglar state it best in Born to Win: "People who make good decisions can test the information they get and filter out the parts that are not true. This ability leads to the skill of good decision making."

It's important to understand that even though it's OUR intuition to "own," intuition can be infiltrated or shut down by lies. (Just like a house we own could be broken into by thieves that steal our treasures.)

The block can be lies we tell ourselves that cloud our intuition or lies outside of us that cloud it. Other people's stories, their untruths and opinions, the news media, and even beings we may not detect with our eyes or ears can whisper or put out lying thoughts that mess with our thoughts and block intuition.

When you decide you want to hear from God, or know what God wants, the lies and distractions are attracted to move in to occupy your mind and cloud your ability to "hear" your intuition.

Lies fear God and are afraid for anyone to connect to God. They are drawn to block it. And that may be because "breaking open" intuition creates a ruckus and throws light out from us to things that don't like light, so they want to dim it.

Regardless of the source or reason for lies, when lies infect our intuition they prevent us from hearing God's voice. And then when we've sought answers and can't find or hear them, we feel miserable, frustrated, and experience self-doubts like, "What am I doing wrong?" or "God doesn't love or want me!"

THAT creates darkness, dims our light, and keeps us from feeling and seeing intuition (getting a connection with the Power Source for Light.)

They (lies) flip your power breaker off, and OUT goes your plug in and your spiritual light.

I believe in the Bible and God, and I know intuition is a real connection that sort of irritates darkness. Since I believe in rebellious beings, I know they have less habitat and power if people are connecting to God.

You wouldn't HAVE to believe like I do to believe intuition could be clouded by lies. Then again, how can you, all on your own, know what is a lie and what is the truth?

So, how do we deal with intuition that is being blocked? **Well, evil is lies. And because it is, evil sucks at giving signs. Evil can't keep the story straight from one minute to the next because it's all lies.**

Signs wouldn't be very dependable or occur at the perfect time because lies are disjointed and not correctly connected, like a damaged DNA strand can't transmit the correct signals for growth.

For example, a "lie sign" would be like someone flashing a "rockslide ahead" sign on an airplane (where belonged a "fasten seatbelt" sign). All that would do is confuse and then panic a person to find out there's a ROCKSLIDE ahead of an airplane! The passengers would know what that meant for the location of the plane!

Or suppose a "GAME CROSSING" sign was on the entrance to a department store. Would that mean the store greeters forgot to shower that day?

Since evil is lies, it doesn't make sense or hit home the way the truth does. It doesn't RESOLVE the issue. It might briefly make one feel better, but it doesn't bring peace or answers in the end.

ALSO, God can REPEAT His truths over and over, show you from several different directions what you want to know, and put the **right signs** in the **right places** for you (and several of them that hit home for you).

God also helps you recognize His truth and your truths, then gives you the vision to SEE the signs that are put before you. God's eyeballs focus your intuition's eyeballs. It's like having laser binoculars that would turn automatically to wildlife, or a camera lens that turns the camera toward the perfect shot you want to capture.

Why does learning how intuition works for you take patience? One reason is that evil doesn't want you to be patient. Thus, the first flipping thing that flies into your mind may not be intuition. It may be an impulse, habit, or an old lie you believe.

Figuring out if a thought or sign is intuition (a God connection) takes practice, testing, and discernment. Like a machine that gums up its parts when it's not been used for a long time, your intuition needs to be recognized (walk up to the key and turn it), started up, RIDDEN (used), and maintained.

If it just sits there unused, it gets gummed up and rusts. Suppose you buy a new car but park it in the garage because you want to save it to use someday. The car sits there, and because the engine isn't run, the oil drains into the oil pan and eventually gets hard. There's moisture ("noise"/contamination) in the air, so soon the metal parts inside the engine get damp.

If this goes on long enough, the engine starts to rust and get stuck in place. That's because there are no fluids circulating on the parts or heat to help them circulate and keep them lubricated, interacting with each other, to stay cleaned off and work together.

Having intuition, but never being told you have it, CAN cause you to park your car and not use it. This is ESPECIALLY true if you've never been told you have a garage with a car in it that's YOURS to drive!

In the hereafter, intuition is dominant and easier to recognize. But here on Earth, ego often runs the show, if we allow it to. Plus, all the lies surrounding us may distract us from connecting with our intuition or fail to recognize we have it "sitting around!"

You have intuition, whether you always recognize it (and whether or not you even believe you have it). Just because you don't notice it now doesn't mean you never will, either.

On the flip side, assuming your intuition is perfect, assuming you don't need any more practice to develop your discernment to tell intuition from lies, is also a misconception.

These are both extremes, and neither denial nor overconfidence are accurate or dependable uses of intuition. Intuition is a skill, and a fine machine. Developing it takes starting it up, practice driving it, and frequent use.

Chapter Summary

- Intuition is a native skill that needs nurtured and used. Acknowledge it exists and learn to trust it.

- Test what you're told—see if it's true or not. It may not come true right then. It might come true in the future, so don't judge it. But discern it.

- Intuition can be destroyed, distracted, and misused by "dark" influences of others. Whether it's people intentionally being unkind, people who don't mean to hurt us, or actual spiritual beings who rebelled from God, their influence can overwhelm or cover up our intuition receptors.

CHAPTER 5: Why Find God?

MORE QUESTIONS!

This time God asked me the questions!

1. How do you, and how did others, discern Me from other thoughts and voices?

2. WHEN and HOW did you find Me when you REALLY needed to?

3. What was your state of mind or situation that led you to seek Me?

4. What were the stories in Bible lives you want to share?

I could not answer Question 1, how do we tell God from other thoughts, because how I discerned God doesn't matter until I uncover WHY I did it. A person needs a WHY before it's worth the WORK of figuring out how to do anything!

I must start with QUESTION 3: What was my state of mind that led me to seek God? What made me think I HAD TO, that I had no choice?

Hey, I've gone to church off/on since I was a kid, and when a teen I went up to the altar and accepted Jesus Christ as my personal Savior. I THOUGHT that covered every sin, if I repented when I made a mistake or rebelled from being good for a while.

So, why in the Sam Hill did I need to "find" God? (The "how" seemed to be the altar call, so what was I still missing?) I didn't know. I do know I was AFRAID of God because, according to the Old Testament of the Bible, God wiped out societies who "did evil in the sight of The LORD."

Part of WHY I sought God was to DEFINE God differently. He had names already. They called Him "The LORD" in English. In Hebrew they call Him "The Name" (HaShem). These were words they used to avoid typing or saying, "I AM" (YHWH) for fear of "using YHWH's name in vain."

If one can't even get God's Name right (or dares not say it) and we need Jesus to keep us out of eternal jail, WHY do I "need" God? Why don't I just check in with Teacher Jesus and get my licks or get kept from the principal's office?

(I always hated the word "principal" because I was told to remember the spelling, he was a "pal." Our princi<u>pal</u> in school did not feel like a pal, because a paddle stick isn't something a pal does to you!)

If Jesus was the one who took my licks, WHY should I hang out with the principal? Jesus is the intercessor, they say, so having to hang out with the Big Dude must mean I was either in BIG trouble OR a brownnoser who went behind Jesus' and others back to snitch on others to try and get in good with the enforcer of the rules.

This flawed logic was because I didn't understand language or the intent of redemption and salvation. I didn't understand Who God really is! I didn't have my WHY or HOW because I didn't know WHAT I was really seeking.

Answers to Questions 1, 2, and 3 came after I realized Who God Is:

God is not the principal! He is not the enforcer of rules. God is the principle. Definition principle - The fundamental, primary, or general law or truth from which others are derived.

I sought to find THE God (not just the intercessor who helps us connect with God's power and healing) for two reasons:

Number one, because I was told to (by Jesus). When I asked Him what to do next, Jesus said, "Go find Him!!"

Number two, because I was curious what this Him was like and why Jesus said that! I knew I needed to get to know God to understand God, the way Jesus understands Him.

I took that step. I obeyed and trusted Jesus. I sought God not for forgiveness or help, but to understand Him. Understanding God requires first understanding Jesus' roll.

Jesus of Nazareth, the crucified and then resurrected God Man (part God, part human) MERGED God and mankind to make them compatible (again) with each other. To do that and root out the disconnect, it had to be without the corrupting influence of rebellion/rejecting God. Because rejecting God takes away our ability to connect to God! It blocks us from existing in healthy and healing ways.

Jesus healed that connection (once and for all). He's the electrician who replaced the faulty line! That's why He's called "the Way to the Father." He protects and maintains the line and prevents corrosion. **Jesus makes our spiritual connection to God "incorruptible."**

BUT, what good does it do to heal a connection if people never use it? What if people don't realize the Lights ARE restored, the switch is there. They don't look for it in the dark. They don't flip it. Something deep inside them still thinks the Power is out, so they don't bother flipping the switch.

I remember a situation in my life where I knew the power was out but didn't want to find the switch. It was when God told me to sign up my family for internet services (early in the digital era). I told God no. I DID NOT WANT to pay the monthly fee and DID NOT SEE why my family needed it. This was when the kids were young, before cell phones and laptops and all that.

I didn't WANT to do it and fought the idea. I refused to go to a local office and sign up. But I felt this PERSISTENT urge to sign up that was hard to ignore. THAT was "God knocking."

He was teaching me His Voice and preparing me to look back on the temptation of disobedience.

It turns out my children were about to remotely communicate in chats with people they needed for their futures to unfold. I couldn't see out ahead of this into the technology age, or see the opportunities they had coming, but God COULD! Since He repeated the internet request frequently, I caved and signed up for the internet (to shut Him up).

Remember those words Jesus said about "knock and the door will be opened?" And that if someone knocks long enough, you'll get up and open the door JUST to stop them, and give them more than they asked for to get rid of them?

I DID it in reverse. I obeyed to SHUT GOD UP, because His Voice was all I seemed able to "hear" in my mind. If I tried to overshadow it, it came back like a boomerang. The harder I "threw" God's "suggestion" away from me, the quicker it came back around!

What happened because of my obedience to sign up to the internet? One of our children chatted with friends in Europe and ended up traveling to Sweden and Switzerland right out of college, having families to stay with. Then her sister visited Europe with her on a second trip! They got amazing experiences because of the internet connections they formed.

And BECAUSE I obeyed God, we kept up with technology that gave them computer skills and places to do homework. This boost led one to an Information Technology degree and another is a Computer Science graduate. I see now it was a no brainer, and God knew it, but I didn't. I was trying to "save money" at the expense of at least 4 people's careers or social experiences!

TO SUMMARIZE: Because I LISTENED to Jesus and went out to FIND God myself, God's Voice became more familiar in my head, and I could tell it from my own voice/doubts/fears.

NOW I'm ready to answer Question 1 in this chapter:

How did I discern God from other voices? It started with Jesus. He taught me by preparing me to hear God. ("Hearing" God meant housing a piece of God in my mind.)

And another thing about God's Voice. What STOPPED my rebellion about signing up for the internet was that God's Voice had **repeatedly** said (quietly but repeating it over later), "Sign up today!" God said "TODAY" because He knew if I procrastinated, I would talk myself out of it, lose my nerve, make up excuses, and possibly never do it.

WHY Seek God? And how?

Seek God because He's smart and the origin of life. No one (absolutely no one, not even the Son of God) knows you, what you need, what your hidden skills are, what you desire, and HOW to help you achieve what you want like THE God does. NO ONE.

It is true that "all authority in Heaven and Earth has been given" to God's Son. Authority is one thing. Knowing EVERYTHING and being a Source for it to help others? THAT's God Almighty.

Don't believe me, Christians? Why when Jesus was called "great" did He say, "Why do you call me great? Only God is great!" He said it because if they saw something great in Him, it meant God the Father was with and in Him. And in Jesus' heart, He wants to reconcile (make people friends with and family to) God. It's Jesus' desire!

Mediators don't want to marry the couples they help. They want to mend it between them so they can love each other with trust. Intercessors (people who defend others from charges) don't want the client to need them forevermore. They want their clients set free.

Jesus is here to reunite people to God and to be friends with us. We are Jesus' buddies, and He loves seeing us with and introducing us to God (again, if we once knew God and forgot).

Moses' Burning Bush and Adam's Staff

When Moses went back to Egypt (where he was a prince raised by a previous Pharaoh's daughter), he went there to tell Pharaoh that his God (YHWH) is THE One True God. Moses said that YHWH is above and more powerful than any god or animal or image worshiped.

And this Most Powerful Being sent Moses to say, "Pharaoh, set My people free!" To convince Pharaoh, God let Moses show signs. Moses carried a staff, and one of the signs was Moses threw his staff down, and it turned into a serpent. But when he picked it back up, it became a staff again.

Pharaoh had magicians in his service for entertainment. The sorcerer magician who led Pharaoh's entertainment asked to be given a chance. The next day he put on a show, and he, too, appeared to drop a staff and exchange it for a serpent he'd hidden nearby no one could see, which he then picked up.

Thus, Pharaoh was led by a trick to doubt God's sovereignty.

What was there about Moses' staff that allowed it to perform a physiological transition only possible to imitate, not to recreate?

The staff came from the same place as Moses' mission: Mr. Burning Bush. Throughout the generations since the beginning in Eden, God had given "created humans" (beings with God's eternal breath of Life) the ability to harness His power.

Adam was the first to receive this staff, and with it he controlled the animals. Adam passed it down to his offspring, and this is how Noah was able to control the animals and gather them into the ark.

It was then Abraham's turn, and this time it brought him great cooperation, wealth, and trust from others as he traveled (people from many races and backgrounds).

Eventually it became Moses' staff, a focal point through which God's power flowed. Just holding it required faith for it to transmit. And that day at the burning bush when God spoke in a way Moses could see His energy, God passed the staff to Moses.

Why connect to God? Because God has power that is not a trick or imitation. God's power is the real thing. It is often mimicked, but the results the imitations make in the world are cheap compared to the powerful impact of God's True Strength.

CHAPTER 6: Learning to Trust Yourself

I wanted to serve clients to follow my calling, but something was holding me back. I was AFRAID to have clients because I thought I'd let them down.

Society, religion, governments, workplaces, family, mothers, fathers, or "friends" can let people down. I was sure I'd let them down, too. It was safer to avoid them. But I was motivated to serve, despite my fear, as if I couldn't let the thought go, like "Sign up today" for the internet.

I was also moved to serve by the experiences of Jesus and His (human) family. Before reading about Jesus' life, I felt limited to what I'd been taught, what my family was used to me acting like, and what they once thought of me. But Jesus didn't let family limit Him.

In Mark 3:13-19 Jesus had just LEFT His human family to begin His spiritual calling:

Jesus Calls His Twelve Followers

He went up on a mountain and called those He wanted. They followed Him. He picked out twelve followers to be with Him so He might send them out to preach. They would have the right and the power to heal diseases and to put out demons.

Jesus gave Simon another name, Peter. James and John were brothers. They were the sons of Zebedee. He named them Boanerges, which means, The Sons of Thunder.

The others were Andrew, Philip, Bartholomew, Matthew, Thomas, James the son of Alphaeus, Thaddaeus, Simon the Canaanite, and Judas Iscariot. Judas was the one who handed Jesus over to be killed.

God did not choose the apostles–Jesus did. He called them to Himself, and they came! He chose them, and they CHOSE to be with Him. Jesus chose to serve, chose to have clients, and the disciples were drawn to learn from Jesus and serve His clients.

Then Jesus gave them SPECIFIC powers and some new names with powerful meanings. He recognized who they really were and acknowledged it by renaming them.

The powers He granted them were the powers God gave Jesus the authority to grant. The ability to do all this and make decisions was built into Jesus. He was born to be who He needed to be to serve. God even gave Jesus the right to choose his own betrayer, and Jesus knew WHO to choose.

In other words, Jesus was born with the eternal empathic abilities to KNOW people and to HEAR God's voice in ANY noise. He had the ability, AND He knew He had the connection, to be eternal on earth.

To "be eternal" means to have God-given rights and abilities, the right to make choices, the power to follow up, and the ability to draw to one the people God chose to draw near Him.

THAT's what I learned from Jesus that applies to me and others. And that's what made me realize that WHO I CHOOSE and those WHO CHOOSE ME are my tribe. Those called and drawn to me are doing it by free will and because God knows it's right for them.

What is already assigned to us by God is ready for us—the tools, skills, gifts, and desires to BE us and DO what we long to do are waiting for us.

Even the one who betrayed Jesus was prepared in advance for the desires to carry it out. Some of OUR betrayers are chosen in advance and equipped to irritate us, frustrate us, accuse us, or leave us.

But even when we find those we're here to serve or work with, other things can block them and us: traditions and family expectations. Jesus faced that, too. Assumptions of others almost SHUT DOWN Jesus and his disciples' missions on earth.

Jesus Accused by His Family and by Teachers of the Law (Mark 3:20-34)

Then Jesus entered a house, and again a crowd gathered, so that he and his disciples were not even able to eat.

When his family heard about this (He was attracting a crowd), they went (left home and headed to that house) to take charge (control) of him, for they said, "He is out of his mind."

And the teachers of the law who came down from Jerusalem said, "He is possessed by Beelzebub! By the prince of demons, he is driving out demons."

The first time Jesus' family turned on Him is when they found out He had an audience. They wanted to SHUT HIM UP before He embarrassed or discredited them in the church and in the community.

They knew the lawgivers would hear about it and accuse him, so they headed down to where Jesus was staying to get Him out of sight.

Then Jesus' mother and brothers arrived. Standing outside, they sent someone in to call him. A crowd was sitting around him, and they told him, "Your mother and brothers are outside looking for you."

"Who are my mother and my brothers?" Jesus asked. Then he looked at those seated in a circle around him and said, "Here are my mother and my brothers! Whoever does God's will is my brother and sister and mother."

Human connections are not always the most important ones. I've accepted that the fear of not "fitting in" (with family, church/religion, or other people) can make us feel ostracized or misunderstood. This feeling of isolation or frustration about what people assume can make us avoid being who we really are.

Jesus didn't do that, but sometimes we do unless we're aware of it. This can happen at any gathering we THINK we MUST attend or fit into (change or pretend to be something we're not).

I've felt like a "victim" at many work or social gatherings because **I did NOT understand that I am "different."**

My daughter, Andrea, was teaching at an Unstoppable Influence Academy™ training program in 2022, and it hit me why I felt out of place with others sometimes.

She said, "They were each unique and didn't know it." (©Andrea Dell, ©High Octane Marketing, LLC, and Unstoppable Influence Academy™)

I realized people who are drawn to me may have the same confusion: We thought we could or should "fit in," but we were designed to NEVER fit in or cram ourselves in some slot, box, or expectation of someone else.

We didn't know this, so it grieved us not to "fit in." Still, discomfort or not, we couldn't do it. We preferred to feel alone OR unwillingly got left alone, because we didn't know who we really were, so we could find people we relate to!

For a LONG TIME, I didn't want to help people who needed me. I was afraid I'd not be there for them. But I forgot I don't need to be because God already is. That's the point—many are ostracized weirdos because Almighty God is close to and inside them, and that scares people who don't understand them.

ASK MOSES

The Israelite people, after being freed from slavery in Egypt, did not WANT to go up on the mountain with God. It was too Light there, which scared them. So, they begged Moses to go and leave them behind.

The Light of God that shined into them made them uncomfortable. It made them seem stronger and better than they felt, after 400 years of being slaves to others.

They didn't recognize who they REALLY were, so when they saw a reflection of who they were in God's Light, it terrified them.

The Israelites were used to being slaves, to being beaten up if they messed up and having freedoms be for someone else. When SUDDENLY set free, they wanted to rush back to a comfort zone. They had NO IDEA how to be "free."

SO, to help themselves go back to feeling helpless, they found fault with Moses and grumbled about God, both to Moses' face and behind his back. They also resented him for being able to stand (with) God **when they were afraid to face God**.

My clients and my friends want to stand with God. They don't always realize it, because they sense the resentment or distrust thrown at them from people afraid to meet God.

Being afraid to stand with God is partly a fear of being controlled (an E.G.O. trick, which means "edge God out."). They dread that God will ask them or show them the next step, and it will be too outside their comfort zones.

Or they fear they won't DO it and then will feel bad, guilty, condemned, and "screwed" (in trouble with God, who they think will desert them). It's because they forget that God doesn't betray or distrust unjustly like people do.

Another reason people don't "go up on the mountain with God," like Moses did, is they think they are doing enough to be good with God, and these familiar efforts are all they are willing to consider.

My clients and friends face the "downside" to following or seeking God and recognizing/using intuition: They are ostracized, accused, misunderstood, questioned, given "advice," and have their decisions questioned EVEN WHEN God and Intuition line up!

It's something one must be willing to face. Over time, as you get secure in your God connection, people stop noticing you're different because you've ACCEPTED yourself and are not giving off "scared" energy. They simply do not notice you anymore!

But sometimes they do! And when they do and they interject themselves to "take over" that connection, it becomes an irritation to you, and you end up shutting down your contact with them or closing it off at that moment. It begins to BUG YOU too much to put up with it.

CHAPTER 7: Creating Joseph, Thank God!

It took a LOT of effort and impossible events for Joseph to even exist!

His genealogy is:

>Great Grandparents: Abraham and Sarah
>Grandparents: Isaac and Rebekah
>Parents: Jacob and Rachel

His great grandparents, Abraham and Sarah, lived in the land of Nun, but when Abraham was 90 and Sarah 70, they had no children (let alone grandchildren)!!

Abraham could "hear" God because of his faith, so he had tested his intuition and learned to recognize God's Voice. He'd even met with angels of The LORD on earth.

When God told Abraham to pack up his family and all his belongings and HIT THE ROAD—move out of town from where he'd been all his life, he did so. He took Sarah, his wife, with all their possessions and properties, and away they went.

God had promised Abraham offspring more numerous than the sands of the sea or the stars in the sky, yet they had no children! They did have a nephew, Lot, so they took him and his family with them.

Eventually Abraham and Sarah did have a son named Isaac. It seemed laughably impossible at the time because Sarah was over 70 and Abraham over 90 when they received that promise!

But they did have a son, and when Isaac was older, God told Abraham to take Isaac up a mountain to an altar and sacrifice him, to prove that Abraham trusted God. Abraham DID as God instructed! He packed up the mule, took his assistant along, and headed for that mountain with his son.

WHY did he agree to such a crazy thing? Abraham trusted his "intuition" because he KNEW it was THE God who told him to do this thing!

And it's not often taught, but AS Abraham left his pack string and assistant and went up on that mountain with Isaac to offer (kill) his son to give him to God, He said to his assistant, **"Watch my things until WE come back."**

"We." Abraham believed if he obeyed, God would resurrect Isaac from the dead and send him back down the mountain with his dad! See, Abraham KNEW God well. He knew no matter WHAT happened, if he obeyed God, his son would live.

As he raised his knife to give his son to God, God said, "STOP!" A traditional sacrifice, a ram, was caught in a bush yonder. God said, "You have proved your faith in Me by your willingness to withhold nothing from Me."

That is, you trust Me, Abraham, because you even trust your son with Me. And the ram took Isaac's place.

What About Joseph?

Isaac went on to marry a beautiful and brilliant woman named Rebekah, and they had two children, Esau and Jacob. Jacob is the father of Joseph.

Joseph's family drama is all WRAPPED UP in what happened to his father, Jacob! Jacob met a man with two daughters and fell in love with the youngest, Rachel.

But because she was the youngest and the older sister wasn't married, their father would NOT let Jacob marry Rachel UNLESS he first married her older sister, Leah. Jacob adored Rachel so much that he agreed.

Knowing that Jacob loved Rachel and not Leah, God cared for Leah and blessed her first. She birthed first, and eventually was credited with 10 children with Jacob, which gave her much status in the family.

But Rachel was barren after Leah had four sons, and woefully grieved.

At long last, after Leah was comforted and redeemed by many sons and a daughter, God felt compassion for Rachel, heard her cries, and she was able to conceive and birth Joseph. She also birthed his little brother, Benjamin.

"Joseph" means "he will add," from the Hebrew verb *yasaf* (to increase), and Joseph was a crown on his mama's head and adored by Jacob.

Here are the signs and impossible miracles that brought Joseph into being:

1. Abraham and Sarah late in life impossibly conceived to bear a son (Isaac).

2. Isaac was spared from being sacrificed and then met the perfect wife who bore their two sons, Jacob and Esau.

3. One of Jacob's wives, Rachel, miraculously conceived two sons, Joseph and Benjamin, after being barren for years.

Here is the SAD NEWS for this family.

Rachel Dies Giving Birth Genesis 35:16-18 (ETRV)

[16] Jacob and his group left Bethel. Before they came to Ephrath, Rachel began giving birth to her baby. [17] She was having a lot of trouble with this birth. She was in great pain. When her nurse saw this, she said, "Don't be afraid, Rachel. You are giving birth to another son."

[18] Rachel died while giving birth to the son. Before dying, she named the boy Benoni (it means "favorite son"), but Jacob called him Benjamin (it means "son of my suffering.")

The Perils of Favor & Intuition!

In the Bible Joseph is called "favored" because he was the first-born son of the love of Jacob's heart, Rachel. But being "favored" by parents is a not necessarily a blessing! Ask Joseph!

The story of Joseph is a story about a man with a LOT of intuition! Joseph TRUSTED himself with God and trusted his gifts, even when it deeply offended those around him.

Joseph sounds like a precursor to Jesus!

CHAPTER 8: Joseph Finds His Intuition

It started with an intuitive dream. Joseph dreamed graphically (Genesis 37, and 39-44), and the interpretation was that Joseph would rule over his siblings, and they would come bow down to him.

He was an honest sort of guy–loved the truth and knew from the vividness of the dream there was something "predictive" about it, so he told his brothers. Then he told his father.

They were all stunned and berated him for such arrogance! The FIRSTBORN of a family was the heir, so if anyone had authority over the estate of their father it was Reuben, the firstborn son of Jacob and Leah.

Going back to the meaning of "intuition" for a moment, what reveals MAY NOT line up with earthly logic or tradition! "Intuition" is information learned by connection with God. It is not tea leaves or JUST ANY information "from beyond."

And the reason for the distinction is that it needs to be overseen by God and NOT be random misinterpretations offered up to "help" people or further oneself.

Even well-meaning people don't realize it when they trust some "light teams" who can feed them bull crap. Anything can "pose" as an angel of light.

2 Corinthians 11:14 That does not surprise us, because even Satan changes himself to look like an angel of light. 15 So it does not surprise us if Satan's servants make themselves look like servants who work for what is right.

If we listen, we can spread half or unhelpful truths to others. The "harm" in spreading half-truths is they distract people from the REAL messages that help people heal people themselves and others.

Chances are, Joseph's family thought Joseph was either delusional, misinterpreting a simple dream, or in bed with something arrogant and evil.

And that is why, when he and his brothers traveled on their father's business, it became too much for the brothers, and they wanted rid of him.

At first, they threw him down a well and planned to leave him there and tell their father a wild animal ate him. But it bothered Reuben to leave his younger brother for dead. And it later bothered Judah, too. So, instead a band of travelers headed to Egypt came by, and they sold Joseph as a slave.

When they got home, they lied to their father, Jacob, and said Joseph was killed in an accident. Jacob was CRUSHED!

Joseph's Dreams (Genesis 37)

Jacob (renamed Israel by God) lived in the land where his father had stayed, the land of Canaan. Joseph, a young man of seventeen, was tending the flocks with his brothers.

Now Israel (Jacob) loved Joseph more than any of his other sons, because he had been born to him in his old age; and he made an ornate robe for him. When his brothers saw that their father loved him more than any of them, they hated him and could not speak a kind word to him.

Joseph had a dream, and when he told it to his brothers, they hated him all the more. He said to them, "Listen to this dream I had: We were binding sheaves of grain out in the field when suddenly my sheaf rose and stood upright, while your sheaves gathered around mine and bowed down to it."

His brothers said to him, "Do you intend to reign over us? Will you actually rule us?" And they hated him all the more, because of his dream and what he had said.

Then he had another dream, and he told it to his brothers. "Listen," he said, "I had another dream, and this time the sun and moon and eleven stars were bowing down to me."

(NOTE: There were 12 children in Jacob's family. He'd dreamed that the other 11 would bow down to him,(

When he told his father as well as his brothers, his father rebuked him and said, "What is this dream you had? Will your mother and I and your brothers actually come and bow down to the ground before you?"

His brothers were jealous of him, but his father kept the matter in mind.

We think it was tough that Jesus' family threatened to take Him away. That's nothing compared to what Joseph's brothers wanted to do to him!

Joseph Sold by His Brothers

Now his brothers had gone to graze their father's flocks near Shechem, and Israel (=Jacob) said to Joseph, "As you know, your brothers are grazing the flocks near Shechem. Come, I am going to send you to them."

"Very well," Joseph replied.

So he said to him, "Go and see if all is well with your brothers and with the flocks and bring word back to me." Then he sent him off from the Valley of Hebron.

WHY did Joseph's father send one of the youngest to "spy" on his brothers and report back? Did he trust Joseph more than the others?

So, Joseph went after his brothers and found them near Dothan. But they saw him in the distance, and before he reached them, they plotted to kill him. "Here comes that dreamer!" they said to each other. "Come now, let's kill him and throw him into one of these cisterns and say that a ferocious animal devoured him. Then we'll see what comes of his dreams."

When Reuben heard this, he tried to rescue him from their hands. "Let's not take his life," he said. "Don't shed any blood. Throw him into this cistern here in the wilderness, but don't lay a hand on him." Reuben said this to rescue him from them and take him back to his father.

So when Joseph came to his brothers, they stripped him of his robe—the ornate robe he was wearing— and they took him and threw him into the cistern. The cistern was empty; there was no water in it.

As they sat down to eat their meal, they looked up and saw a caravan of Ishmaelites coming from Gilead. Their camels were loaded with spices, balm, and myrrh, and they were on their way to take them down to Egypt.

Judah said to his brothers, "What will we gain if we kill our brother and cover up his blood? Come, let's sell him to the Ishmaelites and not lay our hands on him; after all, he is our brother, our own flesh and blood." His brothers agreed.

When the Midianite merchants came by, his brothers pulled Joseph up out of the cistern and sold him for twenty shekels of silver to the Ishmaelites, who took him to Egypt.

(Jesus had one thing on Joseph centuries down the road. Judas sold Jesus for 30 pieces of silver, not "just" 20.)

When Reuben returned to the cistern and saw that Joseph was not there, he tore his clothes. He went back to his brothers and said, "The boy isn't there! Where can I turn now?"

Then they got Joseph's robe, slaughtered a goat, and dipped the robe in the blood. They took the ornate robe back to their father and said, "We found this. Examine it to see whether it is your son's robe."

He recognized it and said, "It is my son's robe! Some ferocious animal has devoured him. Joseph has surely been torn to pieces."

Then Jacob tore his clothes, put on sackcloth, and mourned for his son many days. All his sons and daughters came to comfort him, but he refused to be comforted. "No," he said, "I will continue to mourn until I join my son in the grave." So his father wept for him.

Meanwhile, the Midianites sold Joseph in Egypt to Potiphar, one of Pharaoh's officials, the captain of the guard.

Here is a 17-year-old, the second youngest of 12 siblings, who finds himself a slave in a new land. And yet, where did he end up serving? LOOK where God put Joseph in Egypt!

It was a HUGE kingdom with one ruler. And Joseph ends up... IN CHARGE of the household of the captain of the ruler's guard!

Joseph and Potiphar's Wife - Genesis 39

The Lord was with Joseph so that he prospered, and he lived in the house of his Egyptian master. When his master saw that the Lord was with him and that the Lord gave him success in everything he did, Joseph found favor in his eyes and became his attendant. ***Potiphar put him in charge of his household, and he entrusted to his care everything he owned.***

From the time he put him in charge of his household and of all that he owned; the Lord blessed the household of the Egyptian because of Joseph. The blessing of the Lord was on everything Potiphar had, both in the house and in the field.

So Potiphar left everything he had in Joseph's care; with Joseph in charge, he did not concern himself with anything except the food he ate.

This young man, who was sold as a SLAVE, ended up running the household of his master, because God blessed EVERYTHING Joseph touched. Joseph TRUSTED the dream he had more than he trusted his family ties. He trusted the interpretation. And he even trusted the hardship his brothers placed on him, because God turned it ALL to good in his hands.

JOSEPH'S PROBLEM!

Now Joseph was well-built and handsome, and after a while his master's wife took notice of Joseph and said, "Come to bed with me!"

But he refused. "With me in charge," he told her, "My master does not concern himself with anything in the house; everything he owns he has entrusted to my care.

"No one is greater in this house than I am. My master has withheld nothing from me except you because you are his wife. How then could I do such a wicked thing and sin against God?"

And though she spoke to Joseph day after day, he refused to go to bed with her or even be with her.

One day he went into the house to attend to his duties, and none of the household servants was inside. She caught him by his cloak and said, "Come to bed with me!" But he left his cloak in her hand and ran out of the house.

A WOMAN SCORNED!

When she saw that he had left his cloak in her hand and had run out of the house, she called her household servants. "Look," she said to them, "This Hebrew has been brought to us to make sport of us! He came in here to sleep with me, but I screamed. When he heard me scream for help, he left his cloak beside me and ran out of the house."

She kept his cloak beside her until his master came home. Then she told him the story. When his master heard the story his wife told him, saying, "This is how your slave treated me," he burned with anger. Joseph's master took him and put him in prison, the place where the king's prisoners were confined.

INTUITION BEARS FRUIT DURING ADVERSITY!

But while Joseph was there in the prison, the Lord was with him; *he showed him kindness and granted him favor in the eyes of the prison warden.* ***So, the warden put Joseph in charge of all those held in the prison***, *and he was made responsible for all that was done there.*

The warden paid no attention to anything under Joseph's care, because the Lord was with Joseph and gave him success in whatever he did.

By trusting his connection to God, Joseph flourished and blessed everyone around him! He was trusted and given great authority. FIRST, he was favored by his father, Jacob. Then he was favored by God by being saved from death. THEN he was favored by the head of Pharaoh's guards, and then by the prison warden!

Joseph's story is LONG in Genesis, but to skip to the punchline, Pharaoh himself had bad dreams, but because the Captain of the Guard (prison) also had dreams, which Joseph interpreted, when Pharaoh became concerned, he asked for advice. "Who could tell me what this means?"

And they brought Joseph to the pharaoh (Genesis 41).

Pharaoh sent for Joseph, and he was quickly brought from the dungeon. When he had shaved and changed his clothes, he came before Pharaoh.

Pharaoh said to Joseph, "I had a dream, and no one can interpret it. But I have heard it said of you that when you hear a dream you can interpret it."

*"**I cannot do it**," Joseph replied to Pharaoh, "**but God will give Pharaoh the answer he desires**."*

Joseph said the dreams meant there will be seven great years of abundant growing season, followed by seven years of drought. And to survive, they must store up food during the good years to cover the onset of the bad years. And he presented Pharoah with a PLAN on how to organize it all!

Because the pharaoh was scared, he believed the interpretation **AND put Joseph in charge of making sure it happened!!!**

This young man went from youngest male to despised male to a slave, to the head of his jailer's household, to the supervisor of Pharaoh's kingdom.

JOSEPH'S DREAM COMES TRUE

You can see reading Genesis 41 that Egypt prospered under Joseph's rule and stored up tons and tons of provisions, to not only survive the regional drought but be able to sell food to other nations!

THAT's not the end of the story. Joseph's family still lived in Canaan, and it was hit with the regional drought, too! **And his family was about to starve.**

Then Pharaoh said to Joseph, "I am Pharaoh, but without your word no one will lift hand or foot in all Egypt." Pharaoh gave Joseph the name Zaphenath-Paneah and gave him Asenath daughter of Potiphera, priest of On, to be his wife. And Joseph went throughout the land of Egypt.

Joseph was thirty years old when he entered the service of Pharaoh king of Egypt. And Joseph went out from Pharaoh's presence and traveled throughout Egypt. During the seven years of abundance the land produced plentifully.

Joseph collected all the food produced in those seven years of abundance in Egypt and stored it in the cities. In each city he put the food grown in the fields surrounding it.

Joseph stored up huge quantities of grain, like the sand of the sea; it was so much that he stopped keeping records because it was beyond measure.

HOW DOES THIS AFFECT OTHERS?

Because Joseph gave God the credit for dream interpretations, saying it was God who was in charge of abundance and the drought, and it is God we should listen to, God respected Joseph and trusted him.

Joseph did not "use" God's power to further some side agenda. **He trusted and acknowledged God.**

During the drought, Joseph's family got desperate and heard there was food in Egypt, so they traveled there and begged the leader of Egypt to let them stay there until the famine ended. They did not recognize Joseph in his Egyptian garb and with his great authority.

But eventually he revealed himself and welcomed them to stay, and his father came to know he was alive and rejoiced.

His brothers apologized and realized his dream was the TRUTH, and sent from God to encourage and prepare Joseph for what was to come.

It only happened because Joseph trusted his intuitive connection to God and had faith it WAS from God, and that God KNEW the future. He also knew **ONLY** God knows the future.

Joseph's family, the Israelites, settled in Egypt in the region of Goshen. They acquired property there and were fruitful and increased greatly in number.

Jacob lived in Egypt seventeen years ... and when the time drew near for him to die, he called for his son Joseph and said to him, "If I have found favor in your eyes, put your hand under my thigh and promise that you will show me kindness and faithfulness.

"Do not bury me in Egypt, but when I rest with my fathers, carry me out of Egypt and bury me where they are buried."

"I will do as you say," Joseph said. (Genesis 47)

God devoted this POEM to Joseph, read to him by his father, Jacob, before Jacob died:

GENESIS 49:22-26

Joseph is a fruitful vine, a fruitful vine near a spring,
whose branches climb over a wall.
With bitterness archers attacked him;
they shot at him with hostility.

But his bow remained steady,
his strong arms stayed limber,
because of the hand of the Mighty One of Jacob,
because of the Shepherd, the Rock of Israel,

Because of your father's God, who helps you,
because of the Almighty, Who blesses you
with blessings of the skies above, blessings of the deep
springs below, blessings of the breast and womb.

Your father's blessings are greater than
the blessings of the ancient mountains,
than the bounty of the age-old hills.

Let all these rest on the head of Joseph,
on the brow of the prince among his brothers.

CHAPTER 9: Boundaries

Friendship was a terrorizing monster to me! I realized this after I had a discovery call with an NLP-Hypnosis specialist.

I'd never been hypnotized before, but for some reason my unconscious mind, who I was rarely aware existed, decided to be open with this specialist, and I "saw" something I'd had no idea I felt!

My unconscious showed me a vivid, living, moving picture of what "new friends" look like from its viewpoint. They were salivating, chop-licking predators with clawed paws that reached out to wrap around me and hold me, while their jagged-toothed jaws grabbed hold of my neck.

What followed this vicious attack was that they didn't quite "kill" me, rather they subdued me, waiting for me to lose my will and collapse without fighting into their powerful grasp.

I realized then that "Friendship," at least NEW friendships, were creepy, dangerous monsters to a hidden part of me that controlled my reactions, my gut aches, and my escape instincts.

Remembering this "video" later made me consciously dizzy and freeze in place when approached by friends, and it lasted for months after my unconscious shared it. She needed time to change our mind, and I gave it to her.

I felt bad for my unconscious mind facing that, even when someone friendly came around, and I knew I'd dodged or avoided new friendships for a vivid reason.

But there is help for such walking nightmares. My view of friendship became softened and written over in subsequent sessions. This is something I didn't even DREAM was possible!

Because JUST LIKE THAT, the person God sent to heal my fears, take away my terrors, and clean my timeline helped me write over that belief. She helped my unconscious remove the fear and completely forget I ever had it.

My unconscious no longer remembers the conclusion it drew of how traumas in my life had affected me. Instead, it and I now see friendship as a SAFE, loving, and necessary gift. It's an experience I crave and plan to nurture.

But to have healthy friendships, we must learn the safety and security of setting up and maintaining boundaries. I believe the claws and teeth in that movie were times when someone crossed a boundary with me, and I didn't know I had a right to defend myself.

And during this healing, I needed boundaries in place BEFORE my unconscious mind would embrace its new programming. It needed to KNOW that my new situation of being approached by others would be SAFE for me (and not feel like an attack).

Because until I learned to use boundaries, people who don't know any better could again act like or really be MONSTERS. Thus, after my NLP/Hypnosis specialist unlocked my unconscious so it could open up, it continued to send me signals. "No boundaries, no cooperation from me!"

ALL Things Have and Need Boundaries

Every living creature and everything in Creation needs and has boundaries. "You have established all the boundaries of the earth; You have made summer and winter." (Psalm 74:17)

"And He made from one man every nation of mankind to live on all the face of the earth, having determined their appointed times and the boundaries of their habitation." (Acts 17:26)

"When the Most High gave the nations their inheritance, when He separated the sons of man, He set the boundaries of the peoples according to the number of the sons of Israel." (Deuteronomy 32:8)

WISDOM SPEAKS

"I was there when He established the heavens; when He inscribed a circle on the face of the deep; when He established the clouds above; when the fountains of the deep gushed forth; when He set a boundary for the sea, so that the waters would

not surpass His command; when He marked out the foundations of the earth." (Proverbs 8:27-29)

If every living creature AND the earth and the sea have boundaries, and I am living, I MUST have boundaries to exist, too. (Even when in the grave, the coffin, hole, or box that holds me has boundaries.)

I have a right to claim or live within my boundaries and to respect others' boundaries. Until recently, I didn't realize this! If my unconscious mind had not shown me one of the reasons I emotionally require boundaries, I don't think I'd ever have embraced it.

How long it's taken (without breaks--while asleep, too) to GRASP one small introductory concept on the topic of "boundaries." Accepting they DO exist and are allowed was my first roadblock.

I didn't know this during childhood! No one told me I could say no to anyone. I didn't think I was allowed to say no--to ANYONE EVER. Boundaries? What are they?!

To help myself, I read a book called Boundaries. It's quite eye opening! After reading it, I realized that SOMEHOW in childhood for a while, I did recognize boundary crossings and ran from some dangerous people.

The SOMEHOW must have been Divine Intervention (through intuition), because it was NOT teaching or experience. Often a loud but calm Voice would say things like,

"RUN!" or "LOOK DOWN," or "STOP," or "YOU DON'T HAVE TO DO THIS!"

Thank You, God! I now realize You were keeping me from far worse than it could have been! In fact, I'd not be alive if I'd not heard God's Voice at precise moments in my life.

Once when I was 5, some folks had a relative who was a teen that was "like a child" mentally. This "boy" asked to take me for a walk. And I was used to being walked, but THAT time I did NOT want to go. But the folks let the relative take me off alone with him, anyway.

My gut was right. The relative had no boundaries and started to do things to a little girl he had no business doing. So, my "Intuition" (God's voice in the noise of my confusion and that person's manipulation) suddenly said LOUDLY, **"Look down!"**

I did, knew something was not right, and GOT AWAY (ran) from the danger of what that guy had in mind. By running, I shocked this predatory behavior, because I was headed toward a cliff I didn't see. The teen boy yelled STOP and said he'd take me back to safety, and he did.

That day, God's Voice in the confusion and noise of the situation saved me from rape and a potentially deadly fall off a precipice.

How I Was Trained to Have Boundaries Breached

This part of my history is very personal, and I'd rather not talk about it, but it's hurting me not to.

That day, when we got home, I told my sister what that boy tried to do. I don't think she believed me.

My breached boundary was that my sister can't keep me safe.

My grandfather used to take me on walks. Thus, when my great uncle took me on trips to hunt or learn to shoot a pistol as a young teen, at first I had fun. He seemed nice. But this turned out to be predatory "grooming," and eventually he began to touch me, only a little at first.

I told my mom I didn't care to go with him anymore, and she said, "Oh, but he loves your company so much. Please go?"

My breached boundary was that my mom won't keep me safe.

I was a freshman in high school and my older sister (who's not alive now) was so glad to see me in the same school. She was a senior, being used to telling me what to do, decided that an awkward freshman girl whose was new to the school didn't know anyone. My sister told me I was to be the girl's best friend.

Later in the school year, the girl's mother didn't care for the company she was keeping, so she had her switch to a more popular group socially. Suddenly one day my "best friend" stopped talking to me or looking at me FOR THE REST OF THE SCHOOL YEAR.

And I had focused so much on being her friend (obeying my sister) that I was too tired to make other "best" friends, though I did have other friends.

My breached boundaries were that my sister didn't care whether I had quality friends, and that my sister was in charge of my friendships.

NOWADAYS, it takes a lot of patience, effort, and TIME for anyone to approach me in friendship, even with my brain healing. IF a *potential* friend comes across as CONTROLLING or has demanding energy or attitude, I don't consider them a "friend," no matter how much work they put into it.

I'm DONE thinking I MUST be controlled or manipulated by someone else's opinions, emotions, standards, whims, or desires.

Something in my nature, probably my empathic nature, attracts control freaks or highly insecure people. I am neither of those things and do not care to entertain or have my time occupied by those behaviors. I do not want to GIVE "security" to someone else by sacrificing myself to their NEEDS.

If someone is "easily offended" by my words or actions, best look elsewhere for friends. Being devoured is not my definition of friendship, and I have a sword (words) for when boundaries are crossed.

I wish I could believe in everyone, trust anyone all the time. That's not how life on earth exists.

Ask Jesus.

But Jesus didn't trust them, for he knew mankind to the core. No one needed to tell him how changeable human nature is! (John 2:24-25 TLB)

CHAPTER 10: Unconditional Love

Because friendship was once a scary thing to me, when I loved people I sometimes felt drained. But when I pulled back to meet my own needs for space, often something awful happened.

It felt as if love was a seesaw, where you either gave it all and lost yourself, or gave nothing and lost them. When I pulled back to find time to love myself, people got glum when I wasn't there for them.

Saying no to being what felt like FORCED to serve and love others (OR ELSE some horrid consequence happened) caused me to pull away, withdraw, shut down, and resent "love."

Losing friends (usually by them moving away during childhood) caused pain of loss IF I'd connected on "equal footing" to a friend. Equal means a friend who treated me as an equal instead of their personal servant.

Because they then moved, I became skeptical there was any point in loving, because it wasn't worth the inevitable loss. You either lose your right to your own time and feelings, OR you lose the friend you DO connect with, and are miserable in a lonely way.

Jesus again knows what I mean because He went through similar things with one of His first disciples, Peter. Peter was gung-ho and assertive, and he loved Jesus. His name meant "rock," and Jesus said on that foundation He'd build His church.

The rock had some cracks! Peter got in trouble with Jesus like Moses got in trouble with God. Moses did this the second time the Israelites in the wilderness grumbled about thirst. And God said to Moses, "SPEAK TO the rock and it will give them water."

Instead of speaking to it, Moses TOOK CREDIT (must WE always save you?), AND then he HIT the rock with God's Staff! Oh, it still gave water, but it was NOT God's wish that Moses strike it AGAIN. That "striking" represents CONTROL, lashing out to get your way, and rebellion from God's Voice.

THAT ROCK giving water to believers represented Christ/Messiah giving Living Water, and the Christ/Messiah rock was already symbolically struck in the wilderness earlier, at God's command.

But He was NOT going to be struck a SECOND time, only SPOKEN TO. Speaking represents FAITH. Striking represents DEMAND.

Asking for living water (Spirit healing, cleansing, teaching) was all that is needed. DEMANDING it by striking out is NOT required (and though it might work for a while, has consequences).

Moses' consequences were because he let his brother, sister, and his EGO take over, to STRIKE the rock and TAKE CREDIT for its water. "Must WE continue to save you?!" It was spiritual pride and anger. Moses LASHED OUT at God while taking credit for God's healing work. And because of it, Moses did not cross the Jordan into the promised land. He died in the wilderness, and others led the people over the river.

Jesus' Unconditional Love

Jesus dealt with this AGAIN, now not as the Rock that gave living water but dealing with a stubborn rock, Peter, who also had pride and wanted to take credit and control of this resource.

MATTHEW 16:21-26

From that time on Jesus began to explain to his disciples that he must go to Jerusalem and suffer many things at the hands of the elders, the chief priests, and the teachers of the law, and that he must be killed and on the third day be raised to life.

Peter took him aside and began to rebuke him. "Never, Lord!" he said. "This shall never happen to you!"

Jesus turned and said to Peter, "Get behind me, Satan! You are a stumbling block to me; you do not have in mind the concerns of God, but merely human concerns."

Then Jesus said to his disciples, "Whoever wants to be my disciple must deny themselves and take up their cross and follow me. For whoever wants to save their life will lose it, but whoever loses their life for me will find it. What good will it be for someone to gain the whole world, yet forfeit their soul? Or what can anyone give in exchange for their soul?

What did Jesus mean and why did He rebuke Satanic attitudes in Peter? Two reasons:

1. Peter was being prideful, egotistical, and controlling (definition=Satan!)

2. Peter was being a coward. His fame and hopes rested on being with Jesus and feeling spiritually powerful. If his Master/Teacher was struck down, after he'd GIVEN UP his status in his community, where would he be left? Probably dead, too. He feared for his own life.

That's why later, when Peter claimed he'd never deny Jesus, the Lord said he would do so three times before the rooster crowed. And after Jesus was arrested, Peter did.

Why did Jesus rebuke Peter? Was it because he was disappointed in him, thought he was a coward, or didn't want him around anymore? (He could have sent Peter away if so and gotten one of MANY who'd love to sign up to be with Him!)

Jesus did it because He knew Unconditional Love. He felt God's Unconditional Love. And part of Unconditional (Eternal) Love is correction and truthfulness, because the TRUTH is the BEST tool to use to grow into true eternal self.

Being coddled or felt sorry for OR bowed to instead, or having the lower motives (greed, pride, fear) condoned and enabled is NOT REAL LOVE. Love desires that people grow, choose to throw away fear, and find their way to courage, love, and inner strength.

Incidentally, Jesus had BOUNDARIES. He had a mission and wasn't going to allow someone else' need to feel important or protective get in the way of His important mission. He rebuked Peter again for drawing a sword to defend Him, and then healed the ear Peter had cut off.

WHAT do you suppose that guard thought of Jesus when He put his ear back on and healed the wound instantly? Peter, with his understandable but errant action, probably created a believer out of that guard.

It all happened for a reason, and we're not bashing Peter. We're just like him!

My Unconditional Love

Could I also experience Unconditional Love? I didn't think so until I woke up one morning SO filled with gratitude about how amazing my friends are that I cried for half an hour JUST thanking God for them!

Then I thought about some friends where, instead of gratitude and excitement, I feel grief after I hear from them. Because no matter how much I listen or what I might say in comfort, they show up again miserable over and over.

Their misery drains me if their venting goes on for too many days or too many times. WHY does it drain me?

When it does, that choice feels rough: let them down and fear they won't be okay "alone," so that I am TERRIFIED not to listen, OR feel tired and grumpy afterward, and find a way to release the frustration.

Then what IS "Unconditional Love," that it allows you to be HONEST with people ("rebuke Satan") one minute and help them heal the next minute? And how do we find Unconditional Love?

OR was I being as ignorant and prideful as Peter when I got tired after listening to friends' vents, and I ran away when it got tough? In my lifetime, some people I have turned away from have gotten hurt, sick, or died shortly after.

If this trend is real (not arrogance or some self-bashing trend), WHY does it happen to them? Was it my fault for not helping or "tolerating" their stress?

For example, one time I left a job where a lady had gotten me in trouble (BIG trouble) for something I didn't DO or conceive to do. I walked away from that situation. Within two weeks of me leaving, this lady's sister (age 40) died of a brain aneurysm. It scared her–she thought she was next!

One time I walked away from one who'd depended on me for her "good mood," because telling me how to be gave her something she COULD control, when other things felt out of control. Less than a year after I said no more, she committed suicide.

And then there was the man who'd molested me as a teen. I said no more and walked away, and shortly after that he died of a stroke.

I won't continue–it's too scary. Rather than resent these people and send negative attitudes toward them, should I have loved them? "Love your enemies as yourself, for even the hypocrites can love their friends," to paraphrase Jesus.

Then WHAT IS Unconditional Love and how does one know? I rarely ask God questions like this cold turkey, just privately, but I will ask now because I must know. And when I ask bluntly, God is good to answer (He knows I'm ready to hear when I'm blunt).

God, what is Unconditional Love?

"It is being so firm in your confidence, value, trust in yourself, with the belief everything in you will be okay, that you DARE to love those who do not feel loveable or seem to deserve love." God said.

Then I asked HOW we possess unconditional love without being walked on, controlled, made fun of for being wusses, or being used.

"By being STRONG in yourself and not 'changing' to meet their needs. It is not 'love' to change for people. It is a weakness, and Love is not weak."

God's Unconditional Love

God said no, too. When the early angels gathered together to ask to control earth and mankind's fate, God said no. They wanted mankind to be dependents (servants, robots) because they believe man/womankind incapable of self-management. (They still believe this.)

God said no. He said no to losing free will, because He knows free will generates the only real love, because we love BY CHOICE, even if distrusted, accused, avoided, insulted, murdered, and the like.

To say YES to slavery of others for all eternity IS NOT LOVE.

God knew the hearts of the early angels. It was like Peter's heart initially (and Peter's heart got healed!). The early angels who demanded their way did not heal because they were AFRAID MANKIND WOULD SHINE AS BRIGHTLY AS THEY DID.

And they were afraid God would love mankind as much as He loved them. They were jealous.

At times God Himself got jealous, when His tribes on earth worshiped rocks, the sun or moon, or fallen angels (demons).

These are spirits who parade substitute ways to connect spiritually in front of people's minds–ways that give people temporary gratification.

God's jealousy was because He knew the hurt and harm that would come to people following the concept of gratifying oneself by punishing, demeaning, using, or hurting others to fulfill just any desire.

THAT'S NOT LOVE!

Sometimes "NO" is the most loving answer one can give, to save the person you say no to, and the people who'd get hurt long term harm if you don't say no.

That's why Jesus said no to Peter's desire. A revolution defeating the Romans might have helped people in the short term. But it was Jesus' mission to overcome "the sin of death," to provide long term healing for all. Gratifying Peter's EGO would not have saved mankind's and God's relationship!

God's Unconditional Love is wise, widespread, and to be trusted. If it's NOT trusted, it means one distrusts something in oneself or another.

God wants us to overcome such things as distrust, fear, anger, and hatred, so we have the power of Unconditional Love driving our motives.

Benefits of Unconditional Love

It's guilt-free. There's no fear of being used, uneasiness about caring, or wondering if one is being "needy" and wanting attention.

It's motive-free. We don't evaluate or question why we're feeling it. Feel it without concern!

It grows on itself. The more often we allow ourselves to open up and feel it, the more likely it will make itself at home in our hearts. It knows it's safe in you, once it recognizes it's been there before.

It's healing. JUST the experience of feeling it, without even speaking of it, sends it to the people you think about and to those around them.

It's "credit-free." It doesn't need to be acknowledged or bragged on. It rejoices at simply existing and spreading itself.

It loves being inside you! It's at home there like a welcomed and familiar friend you NEVER have to lose or give up!

Unconditional Love (called Abiding Love or Divine Love) heals automatically. It can flush out impurities and internal hurts simply by existing in us.

It's sometimes called "the glory of The LORD" in scripture.

The Glory of the Lord Fills the Temple
EZEKIEL 43:1-7 (ESV)

Then he led me to the gate, the gate facing east. And behold, the glory of the God of Israel was coming from the east. And the sound of his coming was like the sound of many waters, and the earth shone with his glory.

As the glory of the Lord entered the temple by the gate facing east, the Spirit lifted me up and brought me into the inner court; and behold, the glory of the Lord filled the temple.

I heard one speaking to me out of the temple, and he said to me, "Son of man, this is the place of my throne and the place of the soles of my feet, where I will dwell in the midst of the people of Israel forever."

On earth, the light rises from the east at the dawn of our day. To be covered with it, we must be awake, get up, and let the daylight ascend for us.

Our sun on earth physically represents what our God spiritually does with and for us. The Spirit of God lifts us up to connect with this "glory," the love of God designed for each of us. Our bodies are the temples where God wishes to dwell.

In case that sounds confining, think of it this way: a home with no water, no furniture, no electricity, or lamps, that is cold and rotting, will not be a pleasant abode.

Welcoming the furnishings, energy, heat, and light we need, air filtration and clean water for our souls, allows us to live in one of those "mansions" Jesus promised.

"In My Father's house are many mansions–I am going to prepare a place for you."

And He did–WE ARE the mansions He prepared, and we own these mansions. God keeps them furnished for us (and lets us choose the furnishings).

CHAPTER 11: Drowning in Darkness

Before I share how God's Eternal Voice sounds to me, to the prophets, to Jesus, to the Heavenly angels, and to the souls on earth who seek God's connection, I'm going to be vulnerable about how **"not God"** sounds!

Our mother died in 1978 after a five-year illness. We'd prayed over her and had been promised healing by the "Word of Truth" within my sister and from within me.

I was engaged but still single, with no children. And in August of 1978, the last month of Mom's life (I didn't know it was), since I had no children YET, but my sisters did and lived full time with their husbands, they turned to me.

Someone needed to come and stay with mom at home "until further notice," because she was too sick to get out of bed without help, and could not cook or bathe. I thought "until further notice" meant until God healed her as promised.

Again, my family and my mom's mom begged me to leave my federal summer job and come live there to help her. I didn't want to, because I was building my career and had worked hard to get that job (and needed the money).

I also didn't know how to cook and didn't believe myself capable of taking care of Mom! But I left the job a month early, bagged finishing my last year of college, and went home to help our mom.

More promises of healing came and much prayer. And I believed in a miracle, that she'd stand up and walk and this condition would clear up. It had once before. She was 54 now and first got it when she was 49. It went away/got better last time.

One month exactly after I arrived to cook for mom, help her sponge bathe and get to the bathroom, and take care of her, she became VIOLENTLY ill. She was throwing up green bile and couldn't even sit up.

My aunt Shirley and uncle Pat had a van where she could lie down in the back, so they took her to St. Joseph's Regional Medical Center in Lewiston, Idaho.

My family, our relatives, and her friends visited her OVER and OVER and OVER, comforted her, held her hand, and had been there to encourage her throughout this illness. They also helped Dad, Rick (little brother), and I by bringing food to us at home!

But after a few days in the hospital, Mom went into a near coma state while I just happened to be there visiting with my boyfriend, Malcolm. It was the afternoon of September 15, 1978.

And as I sat with Mom, she started seeing herself in childhood and describing fun games she and her brother played, like jumping out of their upstairs window into a huge straw pile below.

This worried me. She was experiencing childhood in front of my eyes. I got a gut feeling of inevitability and became very still.

But then she got scared and asked me to pray for her. I was terrified because I didn't know what to pray, but I prayed that the Shepherd she so longed to see would comfort her and hold her hand. And when I finished, she smiled and relaxed, and wasn't scared anymore. She was at peace and resting. She thanked me and smiled.

Malcolm and I left, did some errands, and then I went back to the ranch. When I got up the next morning, Dad was sobbing, barely able to speak. "She's gone!" he cried, in the most mournful voice I'd ever heard, because the love of his life had passed in the night.

It started sinking in with me: Our mom was gone. I somehow KNEW this would happen, but I wanted to believe it a nightmare, so I didn't really accept it, even watching Dad.

MY SELFISH, OVERSHADOWING GRIEF

Apathy came over me like it had never hit me. I was a robot who cared about nothing.

Over time it turned to resentment toward God, and even toward those who prayed for Mom and promised "healing." I also began to resent people who wanted to hear from God through me.

But at mom's funeral, I had a vision as plain as if it happened in the building, though my eyes were closed while "some fool" prayed consoling prayers and spoke promises of how she was in a "better place."

Oh, really?!

A moving picture formed over my head of a beautiful, flower lined path, with gorgeous trees on either side. On it walked my mother, a young, smiling healthy lady, holding hands with Jesus, their arms swinging as they strolled and laughed together.

I sobbed with my entire body. Everyone thought it was grief. It wasn't grief. It was the SHOCK of an answered prayer, of her "being with her Shepherd as she longed to be," from that STINKING prayer I'd made the night before she died. She died during the early morning hours of September 16, 1978.

I HATED myself for praying that. I resented myself for "letting her go." I was also a little pissed at Jesus for being so happy, for her being happy, and for God allowing this.

WHAT were we supposed to do now? She was our WHOLE LIFE! Everything revolved around Mom for us. What was demanded of me now that she was off walking with Jesus?

Without Mom no one would want to come to our house! There'd be no more holiday celebrations with just us there.

And what was I supposed to do now? My sisters had their families, aunts had theirs, my nieces and nephews had their parents. What did my dad and my brother have? ME! Me and my boyfriend.

And I had college to finish, but instead I became TRAPPED on the ranch, taking care of these two men, who only mom knew how to care for. And as for the ranch work–I wasn't physically able to keep up with it like Mom because I wasn't as strong as she was. I was not anywhere near as strong or talented.

MY DARKNESS WINS

As far as I felt, my sister could take her prophecy gift and shove it. If serving God means people I love DIE, I was done. I decided to stop talking to God. I wanted NOTHING to do with Him.

And I stopped "hearing" prophecy. I decided it either wasn't really God (God's Spirit of Truth, which is the basis of all prophecy) or God has a sick sense of humor, to take our mother like that and stick me with her responsibilities.

I'm not my mother! I don't have the patience she did. I told my Dad and my brother off. I didn't use that icky "eff" word in those days, but I knew how to tell them to BACK OFF, if they EXPECTED me to be or act like Mom.

And I sucked as a cook! I had to ask her (while she was alive the month I spent with her in person) how to boil potatoes or cook meat. My boyfriend was the "chef." I hated cooking.

The deepness of the frustration, misery of living in the house where mom once did, cooking at her stove, seeing her husband off for work on the ranch and making him coffee, and "taking care of" a spoiled teen brother who said, "Women are here to take care of me!" was more than I could stand.

Since I couldn't stand it, I caved to despair, and I shut down. No one knew I was shut down because I was silent. Not even my boyfriend knew (until he later read my journal and was shocked at the depth of my apathy).

What's worse, I didn't just shut down for that fall and winter, or for the next year. Nor was it only when I really did get married, start a family of three daughters, finish college, and get a career started.

I shut down for 20 years (EXACTLY 20.) It reflected itself in my work and at home. I didn't put my heart into my jobs, OR I put too much heart into them. I'd "look up to" one supervisor and "loath" the next one.

Also, I couldn't "get along well with" my then husband because I HATED myself.

My prayers had not saved my mother; therefore, I was determined never to pray again or hear/speak to God again! At least, I thought I was determined.

IT DIDN'T WORK

I may not have consciously spoken WITH God, but I accidentally talked to God–in my thoughts, in my heart, and in my pleas for help. I didn't think my pleas were answered AT THE TIME. I was hard on myself and hard on God. BUT, looking back, I can see now that God stuck with me, even knowing I was pissed at Him.

Despite my attitude, He protected me. He worked through me. He comforted me. But because I was wallowing in darkness, I wasn't aware of it. It snuck up on me and just happened. I didn't acknowledge or enjoy it.

My wallowing couldn't last forever. I got divorced at age 31. I moved multiple times, and put my girls through that hell (somewhere before we'd had three daughters successfully!

Then when I was 33 and settled into a job in Grangeville, I met Mike Apfelbeck. Eventually, via a job transfer, I moved BACK to Orofino where I had been born, so I could be near Mike.

THEN two years after I FINALLY got settled into a job and we didn't have to move anymore, my employer, the Forest Service, got embroiled in "downsizing."

That started in 1993, and by September of 1996, I'd LOST the career that had been so important to me and HAD NO JOB. Nothing I could think of, short of death, was worse than not having a job and income of my own.

I went through an angry downward spiral, and mine this time wasn't apathy, it was full blown rage (and self-pity). The details are so horrible I can't talk about them. TOTAL loss of reputation, accusations of threatening people, and other depressing and mostly unfair treatment, some of which was FOR SURE my fault for being emotionally immature!

But I FINALLY hit Rock Bottom enough in 1997 to look up from the ground I was crawling on, see the cot I was laying on, and stand up and beg to be healed.

In other words, I got desperate enough, and got guts enough, to talk to God again (though still has issues with how He had handled things).

However, still believing I was a false prophet who'd lied about Mom being healed, I told God I'd NOT listen to Him UNLESS He'd prove it was really Him. The WORST thing on earth to me was being a false prophet and listening to WHO KNOWS WHAT.

So that's why I BEGGED Him to PROVE Himself to me. My proof ended up being like when Gideon in the Bible asked God to put moisture under the fleece, so he knew it was God giving him instructions.

That day in the storm is when I asked God to STOP THE RAIN that had been ongoing ALL DAY LONG AND DAYS BEFORE, to stop it over my head. I'd closed my eyes NOT EXPECTING an answer. Sitting in my car hearing the wipers slosh over and over, when suddenly I heard squeaks had been SHOCKING. When I opened my eyes, and the windshield was dry with stars overhead…

… It was akin to walking on water, to flying, to seeing the Son of Man return in the clouds! It was like stepping into Heaven that night. That's why I'd leaped out of my car, raised my arms to Heaven, spun in a circle, and SHOUTED, "It really IS You! It's YOU, God!! I DO know You!!!

God parted the waters above my head to prove Himself in the way I'd asked. God parted the waters that I might pass through to safety. It was BIBLICAL…Impossible…Shocking!

WHY DID GOD DO IT?

Once I realized it WAS God, I asked Him FLAT OUT right there, "Why did You take my mother?!"

His answer didn't seem pat or rehearsed. It seemed honest and real, Him sharing His big heart with someone who asked Him a tough question (it took nerve to ask)! He said, "I took her because she asked me to. I put her desires above everyone else's this time."

Then it hit me like a flood: He DID heal her, and the prophecy was TRUE. It was the Word of God all along. It was just a different TYPE of healing than we thought she needed.

The prayer answer I'd wanted was because of my selfish desire to have her there to "help" us all the time. I was "Peter," demanding nothing be hard and to get my way! But God put her well-being first. He eternally healed her. He took her home.

And THEN I remembered her predicting it, time after time after time, when she'd said, "I won't be happy until after I die." Twenty years after Mom left earth, I finally accepted that Mom is happy, and it was WHAT SHE WANTED from that illness.

Still, there I stood, face to face with the Living God Creator, Most High in the Heavens Fellow, whom I'd accused so VICIOUSLY for so long. Would He still accept me? Or was I in BIG trouble?

And if I was wrong about that prayer being answered, and doubting He was really connected to me, what was I missing by dumping myself in a dark hole? What had I missed never going out and FINDING GOD's VOICE IN THE NOISE of my own self-loathing and self- pity?

I'd already wasted 20 years wallowing. What had I messed up in the process, and how could we EVER repair the damage I'd done? It was too late for me to repair it alone. I had years of healing to do. What was the answer?

CHAPTER 12: Finding the Voice for keeps!

I am told by people (who know me well), "I admire you," or "I envy you," as if to say "I wish I could do what you do." Envy is the desire for something you seek that's not YET found. It's a longing.

But WHAT could they admire about a prophet who rejected her God for that long? Probably that I sought out the "ability" to "hear" THAT Voice again, and am doing it now.

Still, others may not "hear" the way I do! People get nudges, dreams, feelings, or ask for signs. Some meditate, some get "downloads" in the shower.

Speaking of a download, what is that? Entire concepts, processes, ideas, or answers "come to you" when you're still and relaxed, when not preoccupied by something. For example, sometimes when walking or being alone, things "come to people."

Or scriptures, books, music, something someone says or that you see "talks" to you deeply and gives you what I call, "Realizations." To realize is to figure out something you wanted to, but couldn't before now.

A download is also to see or just know something you didn't even think to wonder about, but that feels VERY interesting and makes you curious to "figure out" more!

I asked my friend, Bridgett, if she also "hears" God's voice in her head, and she said YES! (WHEW! I'm not the only weirdo in the world!) I asked her how it sounds. "Loud," she said, such as, "Don't go there!"

I told her mine can be loud, but often is soft and helpful, to help encourage me during the day! In fact, I see God's plan beforehand sometimes, when I'm seeking answers and I'm open to collaborating.

Before I stopped to talk to Bridget that day, I had this question of how other people "know" it's God's Voice. Then I felt "called" to stop and talk to her. It was a strong urge to stop what I was doing, an excitement to see her.

It was no coincidence that God GAVE me the means for the answer by impulsing me to stop by and get it from Bridgett at her office that day! Sometimes the Voice is a feeling that NOW is the time to do something, stop somewhere, or go somewhere.

Earlier the same day, the Voice told me it was time to go to the store. At first, I argued with it. "Shouldn't I wait for later?"

"No. Go now, within a few minutes," the Voice said.

I went to the store, and as I crossed a corner to get my strawberries, a voice (an earth voice, a human) said, "Hi, Pam!!" It was my brother-in-law, Gary! I'd not seen him in a LONG time! I missed him and my sister so much. I was thrilled!

Had I WAITED like I wanted to, I'd have missed seeing Gary, and it would have been a bummer–a missed blessing.

THE Voice can be quiet if you need a firm but stern command to keep on track or avoid a mistake. And it can be loud if you need to act RIGHT then. It can be comforting when you chide yourself, or corrective at times, such as to help you see the best in someone whose words have irritated you.

Sometimes the Voice shares concepts, not sentences. And I mean WHOLE picture concepts or processes!

Sometimes it's an answer to a question, but not in words. I set down my coffee cup (or my phone) and can't find them. I search ALL over, and I still can't. I get very frustrated (and very blind). This happened last week when I laid my phone and flashlight down at a loved one's house. The harder I looked for them, the more frustrated I got at not finding them.

So, I gave up on my efforts, sighed, and said softly, "Help me?" After a brief trip down the hall, I went back to where I'd looked a dozen times, not even looking, and from THAT angle, my hand was RIGHT by them, my eyes saw them, and they were found! The Eternal Hand led me to what I had "lost."

THE FIFTH DIMENSION

Some people explain this by saying we're living in the fifth dimension, so we have different senses or can rearrange objects. They might say that me getting anxious made my senses weak, so I couldn't see my phone and flashlight. And when I relaxed, I found answers.

I disagree. I've tried relaxing then looking later and failed over and over. BUT if I ask the Voice to help me, then "surrender" the outcome, if it's something I really do need to find, I FIND IT.

It happened this week, too! I lost some tweezers and asked to find them. Next day I stepped next to my TV and THERE they were, where… it seems impossible they could have been. (I'd carefully looked there a DOZEN times the day before!)

Regardless of dimensions, be it on earth or some energetic or spiritual realm and in Heaven, THE Voice's Power is REAL and EFFECTIVE! Maybe IT can shift our location to make things that were impossible now possible. If so, BEAM ME UP, GOD!!

ASKING GOD HOW I FOUND HIM

I asked God why I can "hear" His Voice--how I found it.

"You let down every barrier you had and invited Me in 100% plus," He said. "You wanted it badly enough to find it."

I went on walks alone. I cried out for Him. I asked to SEE His Son on earth, for Him to come and talk to me. I found more than I expected, and saw more than I can see (normally)!

First I had sought help at the church and with the pastor, and I got help with hands on prayer. Still, I hungered.

I sought TOO HARD for God because I could NOT settle for helpers only. I wanted The God (NOW)! Then frustrated, at wits' end, angry and fed up, I drove to the church one night before bed, hoping for hands on prayer.

(Sometimes the building was open evenings for one to just sit and think, too. If nothing else, I could pray alone there.)

Before I could get out of the car, the pastor raced out the front door. I assumed he'd see me, come to my car, and pray with me. As I got out of my car to talk to him, he was already in his pickup, and he backed up and drove off. HOW DARE HE! I needed him, and he left me!

Still determined to STOP FEELING LIKE CRAP, I sat down in my car and looked up over my head. I guess it was that same place I looked when I asked for the clouds to part. I gave God a VERY LOUD ORDER:

"Get your butt down here and SAVE ME!! I won't take NO for an answer!!"

All at once life felt still-very, very quiet. Even my head felt still (no thoughts, no voices). Something seemed very odd. TOTAL SILENCE hit, like that feeling you get when you know lightning is about to strike and brace for the boom.

Then in front of my eyes and overhead, a HUGE light opened above me, and something that looked like a silver, metal, flexible ladder (bent in an arch) dropped out of thin air and stopped right above my car.

Looking back, this would sound like a story of an alien abduction. It wasn't.

Then a "Fellow" slid down out of the light, along this ladder on his butt, got to the bottom, and did a flip in midair over my car. From RIGHT above me, He dropped down into my body! And when He landed, I flew back against my car seat and was frozen in place.

He was "sitting" inside me, and the only thing that moved after that was when my mouth moved with Him using it!

THE VOICE TAKES OVER

The Words that poured out of Him through me (to me) plunged us both into tears! His joy at being one with me "at long last" flooded me with His joy!

That Voice! Oh, that beautiful Voice, and how He feels! And the Power in it gave me a spiritual, emotional, and physical uplift IN PLACE, on earth, INSTANTLY, with no effort on my part.

It was like NOTHING I'd ever felt, seen, or heard. Peace, joy, hope, relief, love, and a feeling of finally being "home" poured into me, surrounded me, and cuddled me. (The glory of

The LORD fully filled this temple, in a way she could not even imagine!)

There, in the blink of an eye, God changed me BY HIS PRESENCE from a DEAD, DARK, ANGRY, and HOPELESS human into an Alive and Eternal Spirit. I was one with God. My flesh was one with God: Sanctified, sanctioned, accepted, and loved.

What He said made me cry and cry and cry. The Voice's words were FULL of longing and emotion. He cried out about how LONG He had waited to come and help me, but I would not let Him! And how He longed for me, how He loved me, and how it was torture to be separated from me. I can't put into words all the words He spouted as He poured His heart out to me ABOUT ME!

I still don't know WHY He did it. I'm no different than anyone else, EXCEPT I refused to take NO for an answer. I wanted God, and I wouldn't shut up until I found God, not until He Himself CAME TO EARTH to BE with me.

WIMPY, PALE DESIRES

We are wimps in our requests FOR God–not "to" God, but "for" God. You must want God to get God. You must decide to NEVER REST until you seek that which you've lost: the Connection to LORD God Almighty.

Jesus set up the Way (the electrical/spiritual/energy pathway, through which the Light and the Truth flow). It's permanent, and we're born with the connection points. But you must pick up the cord and scream out, "I want You, and I will NOT settle for less! No matter WHAT comes my way, who I know, or what I go through, YOU ARE IT!"

Then you may NOT "hear" or receive it right then. But decide to either keep SEEKING or to cry and complain because nothing ever works out, like I did and sometimes still do.

Seek again OR settle for mediocre, give up after the first try, go back to old habits, and get distracted instead of WAIT and persist.

I don't want you to feel bad for where you end up or for what YOU settle for, but for me and my house, "We will serve The LORD!" (To SERVE means to spend your time thinking about or seeking. To focus on. It's not slavery.)

We will find THE Voice in whatever noise. And if it's too noisy to find Him, we'll switch locations, go where it's quiet, look and listen again the next day or later, or the next. NEVER GIVE UP!

BUT, if the setting isn't right, if you must wait, if something interrupts, instead of turning victim and giving up--instead of getting discouraged, GIVE IT A HOT MINUTE.

SEEK AND SEEK AND SEEK AND SEEK.

KNOCK AND KNOCK AND KNOCK AND KNOCK.

Ask and Ask and Ask for Help. Ask for the Way to find THE Voice! Ask for Him to part the waters or blow away the dust storms of noise and COME FIND YOU! And then let Him do it, or show you where to go to find it (often when you aren't expecting to find it)!

BUT!

What if you're not what I am? What if you're not a "word angel." (Word eternal on earth living as a human.) What if you are a dream one, a concept or content one, an artistic or photographer eternal soul?

WHAT IF what I did won't work for you? That what I did worked for me means what you do will work for you! No need to compare yourself to me! I journal and "hear" God in my head because He's cleaned out a ton of the doubts and negativity that used to torment me.

But you have your own way of finding answers! Look for it, pray about it, ask God to reveal it to you, and keep on looking.

Some people find answers during walks in the wild alone, and I have a friend who paints and sees soul stories in people's water-color paintings.

If you're NOT a "word eternal" but are an art or heart or peacemaker one, or if you long after righteousness, then you will be filled with it. If you love and seek mercy and give it, then find the voice in those things.

Some people find God's Voice by helping others share their voice! My copywriter daughter, Andrea Dell, gets inspiration out of helping others spread their message. She's also a concept person–she "sees" concepts.

But you say, "Well, I'm not like so and so." GOOD!

In the Bible there are some big hints! Listen–God had these guys realize this for our sakes!

Ephesians 4:11-12
So Christ himself gave the apostles, the prophets, the evangelists, the pastors and teachers, to equip his people for works of service. (God had Christ endow teachers and helpers, so that we can find our talents and nurture/use them.)

1 Corinthians 12:12-27 One Body but Many Parts
There is one body, but it has many parts. But all its many parts make up one body. It is the same with Christ. We were all baptized by one Holy Spirit. And so, we are formed into one body. It didn't matter whether we were Jews or Gentiles, slaves or free people. We were all given the same Spirit to drink. So, the body is not made up of just one part. It has many parts.

(All these categories that people get put into don't change the fact we're part of a huge spiritual body of beings, here to be spiritually healthy and to help one another.)

Suppose the foot says, "I am not a hand, so I don't belong to the body." By saying this, it cannot stop being part of the body.

And suppose the ear says, "I am not an eye, so I don't belong to the body." By saying this, it cannot stop being part of the body.

If the whole body were an eye, how could it hear? If the whole body were an ear, how could it smell? God has placed each part in the body just as he wanted it to be. If all the parts were the same, how could there be a body? As it is, there are many parts. But there is only one body.

The eye can't say to the hand, "I don't need you!" The head can't say to the feet, "I don't need you!"

In fact, it is just the opposite. The parts of the body that seem to be weaker are the ones we can't do without. The parts that we think are less important we treat with special honor. The private parts aren't shown. But they are treated with special care. The parts that can be shown don't need special care.

But God has put together all the parts of the body. And he has given more honor to the parts that didn't have any. In that way, the parts of the body will not take sides. All of them will take care of one another. If one part suffers, every part suffers with it. If one part is honored, every part shares in its joy.

You are the body of Christ. Each one of you is a part of it.

WHAT IS A BODY OF CHRIST?

Some people aren't Christians and don't want to hear about the body of Christ. The fact is, how many humans have you met who are identical? How many have identical features, preferences, weight, family situation, financial situation, and career paths?

If that is true in human, physical existence, why would it differ spiritually? We all have traits in common, but we all have different talents, gifts, and abilities spiritually, too.

There is a Voice who spoke us into existence and divided the multi-faceted nature of God into parts, to make what's in "the universe," and Who made the breath of life DIVERSE and INTERESTING.

No one can tell you in what way YOU connect to the Energy and Nature of God here on earth. You get to find it out for yourself. To do so, open up and be willing.

I pray that in the future there will be less distractions and "noise" on earth to block our receptors. Because DISTRACTIONS (often intentional ones) cause us to PROCRASTINATE being spiritually real.

They are the biggest source of NOISE that exists, and they are there because certain beings recognize their power, but want others NOT TO, so they can feed off others and take advantage of them for CONTROL. They want us distracted!

Get Lost, Other Beings!

ROMANS 8:31-33, 38

What shall we say about such wonderful things as these? If God is for us, who can ever be against us? Since he did not spare even his own Son but gave him up for us all, won't he also give us everything else?

Who dares accuse us whom God has chosen for his own? No one—for God himself has given us right standing with himself.

Who then will condemn us? No one—for Christ Jesus died for us and was raised to life for us, and he is sitting in the place of honor at God's right hand, pleading for us.

And I am convinced that nothing can ever separate us from God's love. Neither death nor life, neither angels nor demons, neither our fears for today nor our worries about tomorrow—not even the powers of hell can separate us from God's love.

No power in the sky above or in the earth below—indeed, nothing in all creation will ever be able to separate us from the love of God that is revealed in Christ Jesus our Lord.

This is not JUST that Jesus loves us or was loved. Jesus revealed God's love for us. GOD LOVES US just as we are at ANY moment.

CHAPTER 13: Risk of Sacrificing My Will

DECIDING TO OBEY IS A CHOICE.

"Go tell him what I said," that strong and only Voice in my head said.

My mind became a blank chalkboard, a vacant landscape. Every other thought erased itself and pulled away to make room for the Voice's words.

I was at work at the time, and a friend just told me how a young man his family knew had passed away on the weekend. The man was early twenties, and he didn't do it naturally–he killed himself.

They were Christians who did not know if he was saved (if he'd connected to God on earth via the Way). They didn't know his views. They feared and grieved for his soul.

I wasn't sure how that works, either. I did have experience with suicide. In fact, at my sister's funeral the preacher had taught that she couldn't be in Heaven without a husband, because the husband is the head of the household.

This was 30 years ago, and I didn't believe it for one second, then or now! In fact, after he'd "preached" this, a lady was attending who had lost her husband to a tragic accident a few years before. When the preacher made that claim (at a woman's funeral?!), this poor lady jumped up and raced out of the funeral home, sobbing hysterically.

I was so furious that day at my sister's funeral that I ALMOST leaped out of my "family" seating area and burst through the curtains to the podium, to throw the guy out and finish the service myself!

I didn't. I've regretted it since, so at the present day at work when I heard about a young man's suicide, and then heard what God said to me, I paid attention!!

Alone at my desk after I'd heard about the young man, I heard God say, "That young man is with me. Go tell your friend."

I was (to put it mildly) reluctant, so I raced to the lady's room to "think," and (honestly) to argue with God. When I'm not sure what I'm hearing, or don't want to do it, I ask for clarity.

I said to God, "I don't want to tell him that! What if I'm wrong? What if he thinks I'm nuts, or it makes things WORSE?"

"Just tell him what I said," He coaxed.

I left the restroom and walked toward my dear co-worker's office (sweating and fidgeting). Thankfully, we'd talked about God before, and I'd revealed that I "hear God's Voice" sometimes. My co-worker seemed to have accepted it, though we kept it confidential at work.

He and I had a mellow work relationship and talked about each other's spouses a lot, so having conversations with him came naturally. BUT I'd never done anything THIS important or THIS brazen!

I walked to his doorway and asked if I could come in, and said I had something to ask him.

He'd confided earlier how upset the family of this young man was at their loss, and at not knowing if the man knew God. So, I said, "God told me something He wants me to share, if you're okay with it?"

My co-worker nodded, motioned me inside, and looked expectant.

I was scared, but I repeated it. "God says your loved one is with Him. He's okay! God has him."

Puzzlement on my co-worker's face softened to wide-eyed realization, and then a twinkle of hope came into his eyes. As his face brightened, I got chills all over both legs.

Then he said something which was the last thing my fears expected to hear. "I'm so relieved! The family will be, too. I can't wait to tell them!"

WHAT??? I obeyed, and someone BELIEVED me! That was a new feeling. And after I left his office, I sat down at my desk and cried. Then I asked myself a question. "You saw how much it helped. What if you hadn't obeyed?"

I felt relieved about God's mercy and about the reaction my co-worker had shown. I also realized if THIS young man was with God, so was my sister.

I also realized the preacher who'd spoken stupidly really WAS full of crap. Women without husbands CAN and DO approach God.

How that fool justified such thinking was probably the "curse of Eve." But God's Voice had told me 20 years earlier that the curse of Eve was BROKEN. The "curse" had been that a "woman's desire would be for her husband, and he would rule over her."

That was GONE! And I've a feeling the CONSEQUENCE of Eve trusting the serpent over God has been set aside for a long time, the contract torn up, and a new one of connection and reconciliation set in place. Some people just don't realize it.

Because I KNOW that Eve=woman=life has a desire for God, like before, and meets with God every day. She has EVERY right to, whether in Heaven or on earth. And she will forevermore.

WOMAN AND GOD WALK IN THE GARDEN TOGETHER ALONE! Her Maker IS her husband whom she (spiritually) desires, but God doesn't "rule over her." He works WITH her.

Adam or friends are partners/companions. They still love one another, and blend their energy to work together, uniquely so!

And Adam, too, meets with God and desires that connection.

And have no doubt that God decides the disposition of souls when they leave earth.

Preachers, angels, saints, leaders, demons do not.

ONLY God decides the disposition of soul energies.

CHAPTER 14: Speaking of Eve

FEMININITY is not domineering. If we act that way, we are rebelling from domineering by BECOMING domineering. The "feminine" version of domineering is as disgusting as the "patriarchal" or controlling version of masculinity.

Women who long for the divine feminine, to "merge with" it or worship a goddess, or need to declare THEY are a goddess, are forgetting who they are. It's a new type of insecurity, but the opposite side of being the "property" of the (not really) masculine.

The *previous* insecurity was answering to a man or husband, who ruled over her. It was being stoned by people with religious rules which one violated or being burned at the stake for being intuitive or insightful.

The new icky "not really feminine" is dominating masculinity by denying it has power and value of its own, and claiming it is here to serve the feminine only, without rights of its own to exist in freedom.

This isn't disputing that the masculine serves/cares for the feminine and that the feminine feels, is intuitive, is sensual. It's nothing to do with qualities or differences between the two (or realizing we all have both in us).

The original eternals (angels) who rebelled from God, and the incident with Eve, happened because people *rejected* the masculine part of God and wanted God to display only *feminine* characteristics.

God is both. God is the whole. God split out certain parts of self (and of Adam) to encourage the feminine to manage herself, because she is very interesting managing herself, and very lovely. She contributes much, has equal rights, and enriches life by how she chooses to be and what she does!

So, for us to "need" to loudly DECLARE, "I am unjudged! I am unrestrained. I'm unaffected by what I 'should' do. I will NEVER be 'managed' by another, especially by the masculine," degrades part of being divinely feminine (endowed with feminine types of spirit and energy).

Because, just like darkness can't exist without light as a contrast, feminine becomes pale and vacant when ripping all the masculine energy away from her vicinity (or inside her).

One is not dark, the other light. One is not LIFE, the other DEATH or HARD LABOR or FORBIDDEN FRUIT. We're falling for deception again. It's the other extreme of the swinging pendulum.

Do you see it? Woman took control of the situation in Eden to control Adam and better serve him. Adam negated his masculinity by failing to say, "No," to Eve. "I must protect you, Eve. This is not best for us! Someone not authentically masculine manipulated you. Where is he, that I may make it right?"

That's not what Adam did. He blamed God and Eve.

That my husband, be it Mike in my earth home OR God in the Everywhere Home, must sit at my feet and serve me for me to feel feminine is preposterous.

YOU don't mean it that way, but some use what you teach to explain it that way. Some dark entities use your words to perpetuate slavery of humankind and eternals by cutting us off from the Masculine side of God. (More God blaming happens.)

Jesus' mother attempted to control Him. Mothers, used to raising children, will naturally make suggestions to them. There is great faith in her request--she knew He could do it!

But when she told Jesus, "Turn some water to wine now, we're running out," she TOLD Jesus to be her wine servant, to keep the guests entertained (so they'd think highly of her and so they'd feel welcome, both).

Feminine sometimes doesn't realize it when she attempts to over masculine the masculine by telling them what to do. That's NOT the type of "service" masculine is set out to do or be, of being a slave, ordered by a feminine energy.

To ask Jesus, "Do You want to do this, Son?" Yes. To order Him to, no.

Mary and Jesus' half siblings also came to a house and demanded He leave with them, because He was stirring up trouble for the family. They were both embarrassed for their reputations and maybe afraid for His safety. They worked themselves up to hysteria, or got influenced by rumblings of neighbors, and convinced themselves Jesus was delusional and crazy.

He did not cave to either his mother's nurturing pleas or to his brothers' demands. He refused to be controlled (by either masculine or feminine energy in others).

God won't be controlled, either. There will be pull back by God from those whose teachings attempt to redefine femininity OR masculinity.

Feminine ones, is it okay to "get even with" tyrannical religious fanatics who burned up insightful people by calling yourselves what they said you were? Is acting rebellious the only answer?

It's okay, but there are millions of females on the planet and feminine spirits who will miss out on your heart-felt teaching because you label yourselves using rebellious terms.

The agents of darkness who really ARE rebellious (are what you were accused of being) rejoice and steal light when they read your words. They feel you condone their dark activities when you absolutely DO NOT!

The angels and souls loyal to God grieve over those who are lost because they're turned off by vengeful mindsets, but if this is what works for you, then it works for you.

Does it have to be one or the other? How does calling oneself a bitch (a macho, mean masculine insult I've had placed on me dozens of times) make me more me?

I'm not a bitch. And I'm not calling myself one to rebel from a jerk and give them the satisfaction of having been right about me.

I'm a sweetheart, an eternal sweetheart, who admits today she's using strong negative statements lofted at friends, to hope to show them an effect they may see or may not see on how their service is perceived.

TO BOTH MASCULINE & FEMININE

The fall in Eden wasn't about **degrading** women. The fall was partly Adam's doing. Adam left Eve alone with an imposter. Adam may have failed to adequately explain to Eve the danger of the "forbidden fruit."

And when God asked Adam why he ate the fruit, he blamed God (that woman YOU made gave it to me, so I ate it!). Adam didn't admit that he didn't question WHY he was eating it.

So, the reason God put responsibility on Adam to look after Eve (for her to talk to him before acting if unsure) was to protect her. So that someone would have to go through HIM this time to get to her. Whereas before, something went through HER to get to him.

TO THE MASCULINE

Masculine does not own the feminine or dominate her anymore. The "curse of Eve" was lifted in 1997, and woman walks with God alongside man. Any man who misinterprets or clings to the stone throwing portions of the Bible to mistreat, dominate, or take advantage of women is not Godly.

You have a problem if you allow other men to beat, rape, kidnap, enslave, or take advantage of women. Men who enslave and rape women are NOT divinely masculine. They are below animals in status.

And you also have failed your responsibility if you allow others to steal children (male or female) and make slaves of them. Any activity that demands compliance or condones it is NOT divinely masculine.

At the same time, men have no license to take over women's features and characteristics and be treated as equals to them.

Men and women are not equal, they are different. Some men and women are more alike than different.

Mike and I are alike because of our energy types (Type 2, calm and easy going, softer energy). Both of us are also diagnostic and love to fix things.

We have both energies we need to allow each others' strengths to be in charge, without struggling against each other. The heartache and separation that struggle brings are NOT WORTH IT!

CHAPTER 15: Listen for The Voice

Sometimes it's VERY assertive, and usually brief and to the point. There's NONE of that whining, berating, accusing, depressing tone.

Sometimes it's VERY blunt, but not scary loud. It says what it means. God says what God means. God invented language and thoughts, so God knows how to express them accurately.

It can also be reassuring and gentle, or informative at just the right times!

Frequently for me, sometimes it's silent! Sometimes it turns my head or leads me to where I need to find something, without saying one single word. (If the "something" isn't physical, it can be finding answers or hearing something said that I needed to hear!)

The silent answer of turning my head is how the coffee cups and lost objects work. I ask to find them and do not hear a word, but sometimes I get a memory of where I last saw them or what I was doing. Usually not. Usually, my eyes see them when I'm not expecting to.

And then there are the times He helps me BUILD or FIX things I've no idea how to do! I've built bookcases, found out what was wrong with something that's broken, and given people hints on what's wrong, which led them to figure it out.

The Voice in the Noise does it all! It's VERY talented. Sometimes, too, the Voice turns into an ability. It's not SAYING anything, it's DIRECTING.

I've had Him drive for me when I was too tired to be driving, and He's picked me up out of a chair to do chores when I'm too depressed or to do anything but sit.

One of the Voices/terms of the Word of God incarnate (Jesus' Essence) is, "Come on, now! Come on!" It's, "Let's get up and move, even if you don't feel like it." It's the same thing Jesus said to the cripple on the cot who'd been waiting for someone to help him into the waters to get healed. "Come on now, GET UP, pick up your bed and walk!"

I've had a day after much, much loss in my life that nothing could get me off the bed EXCEPT that Voice, that Word (Son) Voice who relates to how earth life feels.

Sometimes Jesus' Word of God Voice and the Holy Spirit's promptings and comforts compete to keep Pam moving.

I must admit this: my favorite is God's Voice.

But there are those He sends to nudge or help, because that way we're not intimidated or afraid of His mighty energy and presence. Whatever it takes that WORKS TO HELP YOU, God sends!

THE RISK OF LISTENING

Hearing God's Voice, deciding to listen to it, and answering the call or doing what it says (obeying) are all different steps.

One can "hear" something or "know" something (that you can't really have any way of knowing) without paying heed or attention to it.

We have free will, and we can choose to ignore it. And then, after ignoring it a few times, even when it comes back around, we can choose to distract ourselves, or flat out say no.

Free will is the right to miss out entirely and screw it up totally, then kick yourself later when you see what COULD HAVE happened, if only you'd have listened. That's an option. I've done a LOT of that–I've rebelled (foolishly, I see now)!

There are RISKS to listening and taking heed:

- Someone will leave you.

- Someone else will think you're nuts.

- Many will think you're trying to control them or take them over.

- Some will flat out REJECT your interference and huff off, racing to get away.

Knowing when to repeat something and when to keep still and watch is called "discernment." I started out SUCKING at discernment! YES, I'd hear God's Voice, but I had zero idea when to talk about it, and when to just keep still and watch.

One of my friends is a wise coach. Her name is Natasha Hazlett (Unstoppable Influence™), and she's the one who warned me about discernment.

The only way I'd heard that word used was regarding "discerning spirits," which is in the Bible. But discerning souls and when to share things with them? I don't recall receiving that training EVER!

For me, it's not hearing God's Voice that scares me, it's knowing what to do with it. SOMETIMES, thankfully, it's obvious and for my use only. It's when that information is for someone ELSE that it's hard to know.

ASK. Get confirmations (ask more than once). Don't leap on the WHIM to share right away and unload on just anyone with it.

But don't be filled with dread, either. Why? Because WAY often I get this reaction: "It's JUST what I needed to hear today. Thank you!"

Sometimes half a dozen people respond that way to something The Voice has helped me see in my life and share with others.

THE RISK OF NOT LISTENING

When called upon by God to help someone because of:

- a thought, realization, talent we have
- words or facts we "just know"
- or specific messages we hear and are to share (rarer and needs people's permission)

The risk of NOT sharing is WORSE than getting in some sort of trouble for blabbing. People can forgive us. They can walk away. It can mean nothing to them.

But purposely running from God to avoid "doing your job" is an intolerable, guilt-producing, depressing feeling that leaves one berating oneself and feeling like a loser. The ability (God-given) to help someone OR oneself by reaching out and not doing it feels sickening.

That's just the effect on us! Who knows what the person may miss out on by not receiving what God is sending to them through us. On the flip side, if we reject help from them, they may miss out on helping us be blessed, and lose out on the gift of joy and fulfillment they feel from helping God help us.

That's not to say we always know or could be perfect. Fear of not being perfect is the biggest block to anything anyone does in life. God doesn't expect perfection!! God has other ways to deliver messages, help, coaching, or answers besides us.

To think, OMG, if I do this I'm screwed, and if I don't it's the end of the world is exaggerating the situation.

God also encourages practice, so the risk of not listening is also never learning how to play, and not getting the privilege of participating, of working with God on earth to help others (and oneself while doing it)!

Why miss out? It's like asking why not breathe in the morning when you wake up. You're equipped with lungs, muscles, passages, air on earth, and awareness, so why not breathe?

Finding and sharing God's Voice (or your talents, images, ideas, things you "just know") is as natural to your spiritual being as breathing is to your body!

CHAPTER 16: Why Be in A Relationship with God?

TESTIMONIALS FROM MY FRIENDS, who shared their reasons for seeking God and what it brought to their lives, are very encouraging!

KAREN KAHN: "When I consider what my life was like before I was in a relationship with God, I probably would not have lived as long as I've lived. Because I didn't have any meaning for my life, and I was habitually depressed. And I hated my life. I mean, when I was in high school, I hated my life.

"And when I came into a relationship with God, I discovered unconditional love. I discovered my worth. And that flowed over into loving other people.

"For me, if I didn't have a relationship with God, I honestly don't feel like I would still be alive."

NATASHA HAZLETT: "What Karen said is so good! These are benefits—real, tangible benefits from people's lives that are coming from that relationship with God, so that someone who may not be in that, or is exploring spirituality, starts to understand it.

"And this is why I'm so unwilling now to say "universe" in exchange for God because the truth of the matter is that with universe there is no relationship. There is no relationship between me and a star or a planet. I'm not going to be in a relationship with my water bottle. So, it's this relationship that's so powerful, and that's why we want to know the heart of God."

MISHA BROOKS: "I say saving souls, and Pam said, 'Saving souls from what? We're not condemned,' but we are condemned without that relationship. We're saving souls *from condemnation* to get into a relationship. And then once we're in a relationship, then there's no condemnation. Basically, it is saving souls from hell, and that's our main goal, right?

"And so then why would we want to have a relationship? Well, just like we'd want to have a relationship even with our husbands, for a deeper connection. Pam said, 'Hell is the absence from God.' Absolutely, and that's the whole point."

NATASHA HAZLETT: "It's separation."

MISHA BROOKS: "And that's the whole reason I even want to be in a relationship with Christ. Because He's our healer, He's our counselor because He's our friend, because He's our physician, because He's our Daddy, He's our Father. Right there that matters to me, honestly, because I didn't grow up with a dad. My kids don't have a dad. God has become our father. He's become my husband. He's become the husband to the widow. He's become the father to the fatherless. He fills that void. He fills any and every void you could ever have."

NATASHA HAZLETT: "We talk a lot in business about the awareness spectrum of our ideal client, right? And so where are they on this spectrum? What I envision is if someone's at the beginning spectrum of investigating, they may say 'I've heard of this thing intuition, and I think it sounds cool. I know about God, but man there's a lot of bad stuff about God out there, and judgment.

"And so many people are seeking. The crazier our world gets; the more people are seeking. Misha said, 'The father to the fatherless,' but until you're:

#1 in that circumstance, or #2 you start to develop that relationship; it almost sounds too good to be true.

"So being in a relationship with God fills a void. And we were designed as humans with a God-sized hole in our heart, basically a place where nothing else can fill it. It's why people are so drawn to seeking out spirituality of some sort. They're trying to constantly fit that puzzle piece that's going to help them feel whole again."

MISHA BROOKS: "And nothing fills it, and that's why we have these superstars. That's why we have these celebrities, and they make millions and billions of dollars, and they reach every goal they can. And they end up on drugs, they end up committing suicide, because they just cannot ... there's nothing that can fulfill that void but Him.

"And there is a song, and it's called The God Shaped Hole. There's nothing else that can fill that. You'll be walking around your entire life feeling like there's something missing until you have that peace. And then it all just clicks in and makes sense."

MAY SIMPSON: "If not for awakening to who God is and who we are in Him, I would have never been a mother. The world displays who we are, but the word of God tells us who we are in Him. Exactly, He is our everything, and in His kingdom, everything is ours."

NATASHA HAZLETT: "Being in a relationship with Him unlocks a lot of meaning. Once you're in a relationship you start to get more of those 'assignments,' and understand that you're equipped with everything that you need. The superstore of everything that you need is available, and it's by virtue of this relationship with God."

ANDREA DELL: "I would say a benefit could be peace. We live in uncertain times, and life in general is very uncertain. But if you are able to rest in God, even with all the poop show around you, there can be some peace in that. And it might be the only peace you can find, outside of unhealthy behaviors, outside of the escapist things we all kind of struggle with. So, peace is a benefit."

NATASHA HAZLETT: "Andrea, you said peace, and you kind of alluded to certainty. Having some certainty, some stability in the midst of the storm, is so valuable. It's like everything else can be spinning around, but you're grounded in the center, so that you don't get swept up in it."

HEATHER ROMANSKI: "For me, it's strength when I don't have it myself. My faith is how I've gotten through everything hard, especially when Grace died. I don't know how people get through hard stuff if they don't believe in something bigger than them."

NATASHA HAZLETT: "Yesterday I was at Bible study, and someone brought up something that was the biggest, 'Duh.' MAYBE y'all have heard this before, and maybe I'm the last one to hear this.

"But you know the phrase that everyone says, which is, 'God never gives you anything more than you can handle?' How many of y'all have heard that? It wasn't until last night when someone said this, that I realized it is totally not true. That is not true at all!

"God frequently gives you more than you can handle, and that is the exact thing that causes you to want to be in relationship with Him, so it is God's strength that is helping you. It's the thing that will cause you to rely on Him, instead of on yourself. And so, I thought that was just so profound.

"I've not necessarily given that advice, but I've seen it given a lot. I guess I kind of agreed until this perspective came, and I was like, Oh, yeah, that's totally not true! God frequently gives us things that we are not capable of handling on our own. But by virtue of having a relationship with Him, a partnership, which is another benefit, suddenly you tap into all these resources, all these things!

"I talked about this in Unstoppable Influence when I said, 'I've got the best business partner in the world, and sorry, Rich (my husband), it's not you.'

"It's because always being in a partnership with God, I was able to recognize the resources that came my way and the abundance that flowed my way. And the knowledge that flowed my way when I said, 'Okay, I'm not going to do this on my own. I'm going to do this with His help."

MISHA BROOKS: "People tell me all the time, 'you're so strong.' I used to hate it because I knew it wasn't me. But I say, yes, I'm strong through Him."

NATASHA HAZLETT: "What an opportunity to let people know that, so that sometimes when they're not feeling strong, maybe they're curious about partnering with God."

CHAPTER 17: How Does Glory Feel?

I used to have dreams about Heaven, and in the dream there was a feeling inside I wasn't used to when I was awake on earth: NO anxiety. The ache in my ribcage, down to the pit of my stomach, disappeared.

Then it returned a few minutes after I woke up on earth.

So, when I had the experience in 1997 of calling God down (literally) on my head, what I noticed after the shock of hearing His emotional response to me, and His GLEE at allowing Him to join with me, was peace.

I noticed, after this powerful encounter ended, two things happened:

1. I could move my body again.

2. Anxiety that was absent with His Presence returned.

I realized later that when God came, Heaven came to earth. And I remembered in the Bible, where they described the "Glory of The LORD" filling the temple.

In Old Testament days only the High Priest of the era could be within the inner sanctuary (where the offerings were consumed by this Power), without dropping dead.

Because the High Priest was atoning for the sins (separation from God) for all the people. And the offerings of their heart– the precious unblemished animals, who were there in their stead, were the flesh that was consumed (the reaction of connecting with God then).

When the Glory of Yahweh consumed my flesh, it booted me to Heaven, like being transported off earth, and I was the happiest and safest one could EVER feel.

It was like being knocked off a skyscraper, and having Super God fly and scoop you up in His (Ever Loving) arms. Then He'd fly you safely to the most lavish, comfortable, well-stocked, beautiful hotel suite that could exist! It overlooked gorgeous scenery, and was stocked with delicious, wholesome food and icy glasses of pure, sweet water.

Having the Glory of Yahweh fill this temple made me want to never move, never leave, and not ever desire ANYTHING else. And to seek Him again at ANY cost.

Allowing myself to be "taken over" free will, my choice, allowed God to help me begin to heal myself. His infusions of paradise gave me the strength, courage, and motivation to seek more of His teaching and healing influence.

God is "addictive" in healing vs. harmful ways. One gets MORE than enough of God, AND craves even more of God, at the same time. BUT unlike false forms of people, substances, or experiences where we get "high" and then crash and hurt, God doesn't leave hurt behind.

When we take a break from God, we use the time to grow and appreciate ... everything. And when we need MORE strength (or love or peace or comfort) from God, it comes to us. It knows to. God knows what we need–He's attracted to what we need!

But unlike other people, God doesn't assume we need something we don't, and push it on us.

I've had people offer me help when I didn't need it. They may have needed to give it, or they may have misinterpreted me. And the feeling of that is discomfort, and a pull in the gut or ache in the heart.

God is the opposite of that. God fills the void that life leaves in us, because interacting on earth as spiritual beings drains our strength.

How does glory (the Glory of The LORD) feel? Fulfilling, comforting, all encompassing, protective, reassuring, joyful, peaceful, exciting, uplifting, healing, and hopeful.

Fill in the blank for yourself because what you need God (and God alone) will provide.

Except He will send others because it doesn't stop there. He can call out anyone and all you need to keep you feeling safe and loved, wanted and secure. He can call out ANYTHING to give you what you need at that moment.

The people He calls our may not know they are called, but you'll know.

Give the credit to God and appreciate who or what He sent. Give the glory, that God brought down to you to fill you up or help, you back to God, that no one will be corrupted by it and misuse the power, gifts, and skills God shares.

We want to uplift one another, not use one another, and not abuse the energy, power, and healing God sends to us.

It will spread (we will spread) automatically to others.

No need to THROW it at them.

OR

To give away your treasure.

IT'S YOUR TREASURE.

CHAPTER 18: Doorway to Crazy

There is room in my mind with a big, thick wooden door that's locked and has no key. My head aches in the spot. I feel dread at approaching it. I can't open it.

The only relief I feel is if I play the Patsy Cline song "Crazy" especially the part that says, "I'm crazy for trying and crazy for crying. And I'm crazy for loving You."

Behind that door are people I've known, and every one of them has thought me CRAZY. That's why I won't open the door. I'm afraid if I do, I'll find out they were right.

Finding "God's Voice" in this silence, this lonely terrifying silence, where I'm SURE if I open any doors at all I'm a goner, is stifling.

I went to tell a friend about it in a voice message, and I kept clearing my throat and couldn't finish a sentence. She noticed and pointed out that my throat chakra gets clogged if I try to talk about it.

My unconscious mind, who's gotten help releasing a LOT, is not at all interested in looking inside this room. She's certain it means the end of me, so she helps clog my throat.

I don't want to deal with this, but in my journal the only thought I had was, "It's part of this book." Oh, no!

I "get" to find out what's in that room writing "live?" No, thank You! So, I try not to write, and Something takes over my eyes and fingers, and we start writing.

WHO'S IN THE ROOM?

My Dad is there, crying because one time when he behaved a certain way, his parents locked him up. He spent the rest of his life running from being locked up. I'm sorry, Dad. Come here—you don't belong in this room now! You're with God and with Jesus!!

A teacher is there, from my first grade. She shook me, and I believed I was the only one who couldn't follow directions, so maybe I was mentally off. Lady, leave this room now. I don't care to see your face in my mansion again.

A lady I wrote a letter to is there, a letter God told me to write. It was God was looking to fill a "position" for which He wanted volunteers. When I next saw her is where she is in this room: at her desk smiling at me, calling me at "dear thing." (Thinking, "you need help!") Lady, this isn't your desk space anymore. You're free to go think anything you want about anyone you want (just not me). Bye.

MY HEAD STILL HURTS but is getting more numb than achy.

Another loved one who got that same letter talked to my relative about how I needed help. You've already left the room, and someone in Heaven has shown you that you were full of crap. WHAT are you doing in my mind still? It's not your home it's mine, so stay in your own space. If you're not sure where that is, ask God.

"Delusions of grandeur," the psychologist said. It was because I said God showed me something at work, and work sent me to counseling. The man recommended voluntary institutionalizing. That's why I love my dad so much. It doesn't pay to be intuitive in this world. "Science" declares you "nuts."

That man should not still be in my room, because his foolish diagnosis got disproven when I had myself checked out. The psychologist he sent me to diagnosed me as "insightful," actually "incredibly insightful." Nothing more came of it. If either is welcome in my home, it's her. The other dude can get the hell off my property and never return!

Some loved ones said I was on drugs, having affairs all over town, and were talking about me to other relatives. Although God completely vindicated me, these voices are hiding in this room. I'm picking up a large vacuum cleaner and sucking them all out, and any others hidden that are loose noise, or dust or rumors or accusations. We're removing ALL of you.

My friend I'm close to thought I was "blind writing" when God first started a conversation in my journal. It was a belief that I was under a hellish, demonic possession, where I'd been taken over by evil and needed cleansed.

I thought I'd forgiven him because, not long after that, God "Put His thumb on" him, and he became accepting of God's will for me. I won't kick this one out of my mansion—he has a room here. But I want him out of THIS room.

Now my heart hurts instead of my head because I feel betrayed by loved ones, and feel I can't trust anyone. The looks I've gotten about my beliefs and abilities cause me to freeze and watch, to brace for an accusation or "correction." People want to "fix" me.

"You need help. Have you tried emotion coding, going to church, praying quietly, hypnosis, counseling? Do you need a vacation, time for yourself, someone to talk to?"

I will answer. I already have help. Yes, several times. I don't have a church, and the last one I had I got thrown out. Yes, hypnosis has helped me. No, counseling set me up for a fall and created dependency, so NO WAY. My vacations are not your business. I find plenty of time for myself. If I want to talk, I will talk. Why do you ask? And let's be clear, NOT TO YOU.

Who in this room were really the crazy ones? What's odd about this room is I was never housed in it. Only memories of what they said were. I avoided it, but now I don't know why.

The door is open and everything in that room we're taking out, opening the window, washing it thoroughly, and sanitizing it. Nothing will be set inside it again, or anyone step foot, except a few tastefully arranged compliments about me.

The door is gone, with entry now through an open arch, pretty and welcoming. It's a study, like God has in His mansion, a place to relax.

1 Corinthians 15:55-57 (New Matthew Bible)

[55] Death, where is your sting? Hell, where is your victory?

[56] The sting of death is sin, and the strength of sin is the law.

[57] But thanks be to God, who has given us victory through our Lord Jesus Christ.

CHAPTER 19: Are Resources "Safe" Spiritually?

Resources, like using the Law of Attraction, healing by Emotion Coding, and use of Neuro Linguistic Programming/Hypnosis/Timeline Therapy™ are available on earth.

Are they "safe" for the one seeking God Almighty? What would Jesus say about this? Let's ask Him.

JESUS SAYS

"If the practitioner is experienced and has the intent to help God heal human minds and enrich human souls, yes. Only manipulation of minds to take advantage of the person rather than help would be called "evil" in God's sight and in My sight.

"I used these techniques in person when I was on earth, and I sent the skills and knowledge of them to equip healers condoned by God and Me. This is to help heal the 'saints,' so they better embrace and pursue their own gifts and use their own tools to help others.

"Hurt and fear interfere with faith. That's one reason for compassion. When people speak, it may be their hurt speaking. It's their mind almost "blindlessly" protecting their bodies from a 'threat.'

"Keeping that in OUR minds helps us realize it's not what WE did (if we did nothing awful to them).

"Instead of LASHING OUT to protect ourselves in response, thus proving their minds correct that we're a threat, be still and forgiving. Or be gentle and help them feel safe.

"Those who use talents such as these in unholy ways won't succeed long term. But God condones the healers and lovers of human souls and minds."

PICTURE THIS

Thousands of years ago, a race of eternal beings (call them angels) were extracted from their higher plain, because they were corrupting that high place–turning it negative, criticizing Creator, and turning many against the truth.

They got thrown out of those 'heights' and flocked onto earth, to attempt to CONSUME the humans they resented, the ones God created to have charge of the earth.

These beings wanted control of earth instead, to populate it their way, by creating slaves ripe for harvesting. They desired to taste of the pleasures of USING 'flesh' (to consume human bodies and animal bodies), AND feed on their emotions (consume their energy, both high and low vibe emotions).

They wanted to create human souls in a different way than God did: without knowledge of free will. And YET to give them every emotion, so that they could 'mine' either pleasure from these minimally important creatures, OR they could enjoy the dark emotions and the power that pride, greed, lust, anger, and hatred can help one feel, as addictions.

They were not allowed to create humanity or choose soul material to implant into humans (for God, it was called the Breath of Life). IF they'd been allowed to continue, they would NOT have put ENOUGH soul material inside for the soul to be a whole, solid living body, and a healthy spirit.

Since they didn't get their way, they flocked to what God had created and lusted to use it, deceive it, pretend to help it, corrupt it, because they were FULL OF lust for control. It was powered by their desire for revenge on God for not letting them have their way.

BE SOFT ON CHRISTIANS OR OTHERS

Deep inside our souls is a distrust. It fluctuates between those who seem to want to chum up to us or help us, and a distrust of God because lies and deception exist.

Why do they exist? So that we know the difference. HOW do you even know to question things? If God had let them have THEIR way, you wouldn't know to question. You'd go along with ANYTHING someone suggested you do or go through anything they said to.

Rejoice that you question things! But don't question your value or let anyone else's question of you sink in. It could be their insecurity. It could be you remind them of someone who questioned their value.

Rejoice also that you can question God without getting thrown out. God never cared that they questioned or disagreed with Him! God cared about what it would do to THEM to never learn that the word "No" has power by itself.

That's why He had to let a serpent be in the Garden of Eden, and why Eve and Adam had to listen to it:

- To understand their nature (that they can say yes to the wrong things),
- To understand and admit consequences,
- To learn confession is healing, and hiding or avoiding is caustic and deadly, and
- To learn that blaming others and God is not healing and does not undo damage, the way reaching out openly for help and admitting mistakes or confusion does.

So, pray about the helpers you choose to help you heal, that they be who God sends, and who Jesus already screened as well-meaning.

Use your intuition and use the testimonies from someone you know. Watch for or ask for a testimony from someone you trust.

Test the "spirit" of people, to see if they are compatible with you, and if your mind or emotions feel safe in their presence. Most will book a free discovery call. If not, look elsewhere, unless you already know the person or trust the recommender.

You're NOT required to investigate, condone, or trust everyone you meet! Even if you could (you shouldn't blindly trust someone you don't know), it clutters your mind to have to decide if a lot of somebodies are trustworthy or not FOR YOU.

No one person has the capacity, time, or energy to evaluate everyone. It's NOISY to do that! It will only confuse you and waste your time, except when you're researching a particular need, to narrow it down to what criteria work for you at this moment.

These gifts and talents were once misused on earth (and still can be), but you do not reject gifts and talents sent down via the Holy Spirit by Jesus and God, just because someone in the past misused them.

IN FACT, the "floating spirits" and jailed ones (those who DID misuse talents to use or harm others for pleasure) would love to block your healing, by making you fearful of seeking help. You'll be okay. You can trust God. Because: **God's Spirit is in your soul to protect you.**

John 14:23 (New International Version)
23 Jesus replied, "Anyone who loves me will obey my teaching. My Father will love them, and we will come to them and make our home with them."

To put it into context in the Bible, here's the entire chapter. Read it 50 times for 50 reasons! It sums up most EVERYTHING about Jesus and God being with us.

Jesus Comforts His Disciples
14 "Do not let your hearts be troubled. You believe in God; believe also in me. **2** My Father's house has many rooms; if that were not so, would I have told you that I am going there to prepare a place for you? **3** And if I go and prepare a place for you, I will come back and take you to be with me that you also may be where I am. **4** You know the way to the place where I am going."

Jesus the Way to the Father
5 Thomas said to him, "Lord, we don't know where you are going, so how can we know the way?"

6 Jesus answered, "I am the way and the truth and the life. No one comes to the Father except through me. **7** If you really know me, you will know my Father as well. From now on, you do know him and have seen him."

8 Philip said, "Lord, show us the Father and that will be enough for us."

9 Jesus answered: "Don't you know me, Philip, even after I have been among you such a long time? Anyone who has seen me has seen the Father. How can you say, 'Show us the Father'?

10 Don't you believe that I am in the Father, and that the Father is in me? The words I say to you I do not speak on my own authority. Rather, it is the Father, living in me, who is doing his work. **11** Believe me when I say that I am in the Father and the Father is in me; or at least believe on the evidence of the works themselves.

12 Very truly I tell you, whoever believes in me will do the works I have been doing, and they will do even greater things than these, because I am going to the Father. **13** And I will do whatever you ask in my name, so that the Father may be glorified in the Son. **14** You may ask me for anything in my name, and I will do it.

Jesus Promises the Holy Spirit
15 "If you love me, keep my commands. **16** And I will ask the Father, and he will give you another advocate to help you and be with you forever— **17** the Spirit of truth. The world cannot accept him, because it neither sees him nor knows him. But you know him, for he lives with you and will be in you.

18 I will not leave you as orphans; I will come to you. **19** Before long, the world will not see me anymore, but you will see me. Because I live, you also will live. **20** On that day you will realize that I am in my Father, and you are in me, and I am in you.

21 Whoever has my commands and keeps them is the one who loves me. The one who loves me will be loved by my Father, and I too will love them and show myself to them."

22 Then Judas (not Judas Iscariot) said, "But, Lord, why do you intend to show yourself to us and not to the world?"

23 Jesus replied, "Anyone who loves me will obey my teaching. My Father will love them, and we will come to them and make our home with them.

24 Anyone who does not love me will not obey my teaching. These words you hear are not my own; they belong to the Father who sent me.

25 "All this I have spoken while still with you. **26** But the Advocate, the Holy Spirit, whom the Father will send in my name, will teach you all things and will remind you of everything I have said to you.

27 Peace I leave with you; my peace I give you. I do not give to you as the world gives. Do not let your hearts be troubled and do not be afraid.

28 You heard me say, I am going away and I am coming back to you. If you loved me, you would be glad that I am going to the Father, for the Father is greater than I.

29 I have told you now before it happens, so that when it does happen you will believe. **30** I will not say much more to you, for the prince of this world is coming. He has no hold over me, **31** but he comes so that the world may learn that I love the Father and do exactly what my Father has commanded me.

"Come now; let us leave."

ABOUT THE AUTHOR

Pam Apfelbeck became a spiritual leader when she went off alone in 1997, to scream to God to, "Get Your butt down here and save me!"

God BOLDLY responded by "inhabiting" her body and soul to deliver an emotional message of love and acceptance, saying, "For so very long I've wanted to come to you, but you would not let Me!"

God then called on Pam to transmit His words and teaching, to encourage souls to be authentically eternal, while still living as humans on earth—to connect to God NOW, not wait for Heaven "someday."

Pam shares God's insights to lead and teach God's chosen. One way is by granting them the permission they seem to lack, so they feel free to embrace their eternal nature & connect to God's power within them.

In her first book, "My Yahweh Journey: How I Became One with I AM," Pam explains her childhood and how she came to recognize God's voice and how God moved in her life. Then in "Romancing an Angel of The LORD," Pam shares how God brought Mike and her together as partners on earth. God has kept them committed to an understanding, appreciative partnership for over 30 years. Pam and Mike live in a small rural town in north central Idaho.

www.ingramcontent.com/pod-product-compliance
Lightning Source LLC
Chambersburg PA
CBHW051755040426
42446CB00007B/382